The

Bohemian
Grove

Facts & Fiction

The

Bohemian Grove

Facts & Fiction

Mark Dice

The Resistance
San Diego, CA

Table of Contents

Also by Mark Dice:

-*Inside the Illuminati*
-*The Illuminati:* Facts & Fiction
-*The New World Order*: Facts & Fiction
-*The Bilderberg Group*: Facts & Fiction
-*Illuminati in the Music Industry*
-*The Resistance Manifesto*
- *The True Story of Fake News*
-*Big Brother:* The Orwellian Nightmare
                              Come True

Connect with Mark on:

Facebook.com/MarkDice
Twitter.com/MarkDice
Instagram.com/MarkDice
YouTube.com/MarkDice
MarkDice.com

Introduction

It sounds like the plot of a cheesy horror film; a group of the world's most powerful men gather in a secluded forest once a year where they dress in black robes and perform a strange ceremony looking like a human sacrifice as they discuss their plans for world domination—but in this case it's not the story in some movie, it's the story of the Bohemian Grove.

Many people interested in "conspiracy theories" about the Illuminati and the New World Order have heard of the Bohemian Grove and probably know a few things about it, and if you're one of these people, I promise this book will be packed with information and little-known details that few people have ever heard. It's a story so bizarre, that many simply can't believe it.

You are about to learn the hidden history, the strange rituals, and the secrets of one of the world's most exclusive clubs. I will reveal the identity of their most powerful members and details of the over 100 different subgroups within and what world-changing ideas and events the Bohemian Grove has given birth to. I'll cover what they call Lakeside Talks which are off the record speeches given by elite politicians and business titans to members in order to give them inside information about the speakers' area of expertise. I will reveal the secret meaning of their motto, "weaving spiders come not here," and the name of their patron saint and what he symbolizes. I'll cover early investigations into the club and the leaks of their membership lists, maps, and year books; I will even reveal their tax returns and financial statements, and show you how we know what we know about this mysterious millionaires men's retreat.

I will analyze the allegations of prostitutes servicing the members, and the gay orgies that are rumored to occur inside. I'll also take a close look at the horrific allegations of murders and snuff films some say have occurred inside the forest at the hands of members; and you'll see why major talk radio hosts and the mainstream media are afraid to acknowledge the place even exists.

The Bohemian Grove is a 2700-acre redwood forest in northern California located about an hour north of San Francisco in a small town named Monte Rio. It is owned by the Bohemian Club, which is headquartered in San Francisco, and their forest—or "the Grove," as it is called—serves as a vacation spot for around 1000 of the world's most wealthy and powerful men who meet there every summer in the middle of July for a "men's retreat."

Every summer it's common for both boys and girls to have retreats in the form of basketball camp or cheerleading camp, where the kids spend a week or so polishing their skills and going through various drills to improve their game. Of course, many Christian churches have annual men's and women's retreats which facilitate friendship and camaraderie among their church members, and the events also serve to further the attendees' education on spiritual matters.

So, similarly, the Superclass, the Establishment, the Ruling Elite, the Illuminati—whatever name you want to call them—have their retreat as well, which serves as a place to rub elbows with other industry leaders and powerful politicians in a private, relaxed, and informal environment.

The annual mid-summer encampment at the Bohemian Grove has been called the "greatest men's party on earth" by members, who include many presidents, military leaders, famous journalists, and top businessmen who enjoy getting away from their wives and the public eye for a bit to let loose and mingle with other like-minded individuals. The gathering lasts for two weeks from mid-July to the end of the month, with some men coming for a weekend, and others staying for an entire week or longer. The men call each other Bohos or Grovers, and members often bring guests with them, but they must be prescreened and approved beforehand by the club.

The term *Bohemian* refers to people who live non-traditional lifestyles and people who are adventurers, or vagabonds. Ever since it was started, the club's logo has been an owl because it symbolizes wisdom since it can "see in the dark." This is because the elite members view themselves as wise and enlightened beings. A forty-foot tall concrete "owl" shrine was constructed inside the Bohemian forest, and every year since 1929 has been the site of the annual Cremation of Care ceremony, one of the strangest aspects of this elite retreat. This is the ritual which they perform each year to kick off their two week long "encampment."

The Cremation of Care consists of an elaborate production involving live music and fireworks— and a human sacrifice reenactment where a life-size effigy of a person is placed on an altar at the base of the giant owl shrine and then burned or "sacrificed." Critics claim the ritual is a toned down and theatrical version of an ancient human sacrifice to Canaanite Gods or the Devil.

It sounds so bizarre, many people chalk it up to an urban legend or an Internet conspiracy theory, but I'll prove to you in this book that such a thing does happen, and the "rumors" are in fact true. In the 1980s, and 90s as word slowly spread

4

about this place, occasionally a reporter tried to sneak inside the now highly guarded compound, but (at least at the time I'm writing this in mid-2015) little to nothing has been reported in the mainstream media about this fascinating (and frightening) forest.

In the past, membership lists and program guides would sometimes get stolen and made public by employees, and in the 1980s a group called the Bohemian Grove Action Network dedicated themselves to doing just that. The membership list, one of which I personally have in my possession thanks to a former employee, has included every Republican U.S. President since 1923, many cabinet officials, directors and CEO's of large corporations and major financial institutions, and top military brass.

Some of these names include George W. Bush, George H. W. Bush, Dick Cheney, Colin Powell, Ronald Reagan, Richard Nixon, Dwight Eisenhower, Alan Greenspan, Arnold Schwarzenegger, and many other mainly Republican members and guests. No current president attends because their schedule and whereabouts is too closely watched, but before and after they are in office they can be found in the Grove.

Some consider the Bohemian Grove to be like a Skull & Bones club for adults, and see the

Cremation of Care ceremony as being similar to the satanic induction ritual that "Bonesmen" are put through in college, only with a few extra zeroes added to the budget. As you may be aware, the Skull & Bones "fraternity" located at Yale University recruits fifteen new seniors each spring to join their club and then grooms them for a possible high-level position in the Eastern Establishment once they graduate. Their initiation rituals are blatantly satanic and involve a simulated human sacrifice as well.[1]

Many people dismiss Skull & Bones as just a "fraternity" for rich kids, but it is far from a fraternity. In reality it is a senior society, meaning people don't become a member until their senior year, and the organization is designed as an entryway to America's Establishment and geared for the students' post-graduate life. They hold meetings every Thursday and Sunday night during the school year to indoctrinate the new members with the philosophies and tactics of the ruling class—where, by the way, no alcohol is drank, or even allowed inside their clubhouse.[2]

---

[1] *New York Observer* "At Skull and Bones, Bush's Secret Club Initiates Ream Gore" by Ron Rosenbaum (April 23rd 2001)

[2] Robbins, Alexandra - *Secrets of the Tomb: Skull and Bones, the Ivy League, and the Hidden Paths of Power* page 130

What kind of a college "fraternity" doesn't allow alcohol in their clubhouse? One that is very serious about their goals of gaining and maintaining power. If you take the time to study Skull & Bones, you will see beyond a shadow of a doubt, that they are far from a "fraternity," and are in fact a deadly serious secret society with direct connections to the Bavarian Illuminati in Germany which was started by Adam Weishaupt.

So the "kids" in Skull & Bones conduct a satanic human sacrifice reenactment ritual in college, but then instead of outgrowing this juvenile frat boy "phase," they become involved in even more elaborate and strange rituals when they are well established adults and old men at the Bohemian Grove!

Is this where the secret rulers of the world meet to plot the course of planet earth? Is the mainstream media part of a cover-up to blackout any mention of the club? What is the evidence for the allegations made about the Grove? Is this annual gathering the Bilderberg Group's summer camp? Are they really performing satanic rituals or human sacrifices? You are about to learn the answers to these questions and more, and we take a close look into *The Bohemian Grove: Facts & Fiction.*

History of the Grove

The Bohemian Club was started in San Francisco in 1872 by artists, musicians, and writers as an excuse for late-night drinking for those who supported Bohemianism which had become quite trendy in the late 19th and early 20th century. These Bohemians celebrated hedonism and overindulgence, and reveled in rebelling against the conservative conventions of the culture. Soon after its formation, businessmen and those with money joined the party and were called "men of use" by the original artistic founders, who called themselves "men of talent."[3]   The artists enjoyed having the wealthy newcomers help foot the bill for their increasingly elaborate parties.

What originally began in their San Francisco clubhouse soon took a more rural turn.   By the early 1880s, the Bohemian Club was holding weekend campouts during the summer in the vast redwood forests around Sonoma County, California.   In 1893 they began renting the location now known as the Bohemian Grove from the Sonoma Lumber Company and later purchased 160-acres of the forest in 1901, later expanding

---

[3] Hanson, Mike - *Bohemian Grove: Cult of Conspiracy* page 25

their ownership to the current 2712 acres [over four square miles].

Most men's clubs meet in Masonic lodges or fancy country clubs, but because of its unique rural atmosphere, the Bohemian Grove soon became a favorite spot where wealthy men could relive their college days of partying like there was no tomorrow. In the 1930s the Bohemian Grove became a favorite of U.S. Presidents as sort of a Camp David in the woods, and this is when word about the Grove began to quiet and the media blackout began. Members and guests enter the campground with the strict understanding that what goes on at the Bohemian Grove stays at the Bohemian Grove, and discussions—whether personal or business related—are all completely "off the record."

The Grove is not "just a campground." There are hundreds of structures inside ranging from elaborate clubhouses and sleeping quarters to a massive industrial kitchen and large amphitheaters —all of which is maintained by a rather large staff, not to mention guarded by an expensive security force and local police. As you may imagine maintaining such a luxurious facility is not cheap.

Back in 1887, the entrance fee for joining the club was $100 and the dues were $3.00 a month. By 1930 this had risen to $500 and $15 a month after that. In the 1990s, the initiation fee was $10,000 with $120 a month dues.[4] There is a ten to fifteen year waiting list for new applicants, and in order to even be considered for membership two current non-related members must sponsor the prospect, who is then thoroughly screened by a membership committee before being placed on the wait list.

Since few men actually quit the club, most aspiring members literally have to usually wait until someone dies to then take their place. Many of the members are in their sixties and seventies, and a few of them usually pass away each year.

The Bohemian Club is registered with the IRS as a 501(c)7 Social Club, which makes them exempt from federal income tax and possibly state property tax as well. One of the requirements for 501(c) organizations is that their financial records are made available to the public for inspection—if you know where to look. I have been able to obtain these documents and they are quite interesting.

The 2013 records show that the club took in $10,168,330 dollars in revenue that calendar year.[5]

---

[4] Phillips, Peter - *A Relative Advantage: Sociology of the San Francisco Bohemian Club. A Doctoral Dissertation* (1994) page 27

[5] Bohemian Club's 2013 - 990 Tax Forms - Line 9

They paid out $3,007,779 in salaries to the staff, and "other expenses" were listed at $2,971,656, which went to pay for the food, booze, insurance, electricity, building maintenance, etc. Their total expenses for the year were $5,997,272. Total assets are listed at $20,428,708. Yes—twenty million dollars!

The general manager or the chief operating officer, Matthew Oggero was paid $556,897. The executive chef Jean-Marie Rigollet was paid $164,515. The controller Michael Boozing was paid $146,240; the HR director Jennifer Robertson was paid $145,385; the Grove Keeper James Daniel took in $146,874; and the financial director Deena Soulon was paid $222,071.

The forms note, "The compensation of all management employees are reviewed and approved annually by the compensation committee consisting of the president, vice president, and treasurer, who also set the composition benefits for the general manager."[6] Each Bohemian Grove member casts one vote for each position the governing body fills.

The first book dedicated to exposing the Bohemian Grove was published in 1974 titled *The Bohemian Grove and other Retreats*, written by

---

[6] Bohemian Club's 2013 Tax Forms 990 Schedule O, Supplemental Information (2013)

William Domhoff, a sociologist and professor who taught at the University of California, Santa Cruz. He starts off the book explaining that upper-class retreats are of a major sociological relevance because, "they increase the social cohesiveness of America's rulers and provide private settings in which business and political problems can be discussed informally and off the record."[7]

Domhoff and a handful of other scholars who are familiar with the Grove insist it's not just a vacation hideaway for the rich and powerful, but instead functions to facilitate the ruling class network and elitist ideologies which affects the entire world.

The book also exposed the Cremation of Care ritual, and starts off the first page saying, "You are one of fifteen hundred men gathered together from all over the country for the annual encampment of the rich and famous at the Bohemian Grove. And you are about to take part in a strange ceremony that has marked every Bohemian Grove gathering since 1880."[8] It goes on to include a full transcript and detailed description of the Cremation of Care, which was a historic revelation at the time,

---

[7] Domhoff, William - *The Bohemian Grove and Other Retreats: A Study in Ruing-Class Cohesiveness* Preface

[8] Domhoff, William - *The Bohemian Grove and Other Retreats: A Study in Ruing-Class Cohesiveness* Page 1

especially since this was back in the 1970s—decades before the Information Age.

Almost ten years after Domhoff's book came out, *ABC News* surprisingly aired a segment about the Bohemian Grove in 1981. Somebody, somehow, was able to get a copy of this report from their archives and posted it on YouTube in 2006 where it can be seen today.[9] The anchor at the time was Frank Reynolds, who began the segment asking, "What have Herbert Hoover, Art Linkletter, Jack London and Richard Nixon all had in common? Well, they've all been members of the exclusive all male, Bohemian Club in California, where every year at this time the elite from around the country get together for two and half weeks of, um, fun and games."[10]

The segment then went on to reveal that more than 2000 members and guests spend two weeks camped out in the secluded redwood forest and named Gerald Ford, Henry Kissinger, George H.W. Bush, Ronald Reagan, and Richard Nixon as members, along with executives at Standard Oil and Bank of America. "Privacy is one of the

---

[9] YouTube: 1981 News Report about Bohemian Grove (posted by user Jaketom3 on December 15th 2006) Other channels have also reposted this video.

[10] ABC News - Segment about Bohemian Grove (July 23, 1981)

Grove's most cherished virtues," the report continues. "Members may not photograph, record, speak or write about activities at the retreat. While many public officials are Grove members, the press is a distinctly unwelcome guest."

The segment even showed a photograph of the Cremation of Care and included an interview with sociologist William Domhoff who explained, "With the ceremony called the Cremation of Care that begins the two week encampment, where the body of Dull Care—symbolizing woes and concerns—is burned on an altar in front of a big owl statue, when that ceremony ends, they all start to cheer and yell, and hand each other a beer."[11]

The segment also pointed out that no women were allowed, not even as employees [at the time], and admitted the atomic bomb was developed by club insiders. The senior ABC News editor must have been on vacation, or the Bohemian Grove became arrogant and didn't think a major news network would betray the strict editorial control by Establishment insiders which usually prevents such stories from making it to the airwaves.

Since this historic segment over three decades ago, there hasn't been a single national news organization that has made a peep about the

---

[11] Ibid.

Bohemian Grove—at least as of mid-2015 when I'm writing this book—not even a tabloid news show. Pretty much only alternative news sites, and the local Sonoma County *Press Democrat* newspaper have ever acknowledged it even exists.

A staff of several hundred people help run the place during the summer encampment, working to cook food and keep up the grounds, most of them local high school kids from nearby towns who have no idea about the identities of the men they are serving. For almost 100 years only men (and teenage boys) were allowed to work inside. But as powerful as the Bohemian Grove is, they were not strong enough to prevent the feminists from crashing their party. In 1978 the club was charged with discrimination by the Department of Fair Employment and Housing for not hiring female employees.[12]

The club fought the charge and in 1981 a judge dismissed the case, but this was only a temporary victory. The judge's decision was based on the members' freedom to associate with who they wanted to associate with and included a statement that since the men "urinate in the open without even the use of rudimentary toilet facilities," the

---

[12]   *The New York Times* "Bohemian Club Is Upheld On Refusal to Hire Women" (January 23rd 1981)

presence of women would infringe on the men's right to privacy.

The feminists didn't give up though and continued to pursue the case. Another judge overruled the previous decision a few months later and ordered the club to begin hiring women.[13] The club filed an appeal with the Supreme Court arguing that their freedom to associate was being violated, but the Court found against the Bohemian Grove.

To be clear, the Court didn't say they had to allow women as members, but did force them to hire women as employees. There is a world of difference between being a member (or guest) and being an employee at the Grove. The employees are mainly contained in the kitchen and dining area, and do not mingle with the guests in their clubhouses or throughout the grounds.

Despite losing their vigorous battle hoping to prevent women from working at the Grove, the Bohos find it amusing that women now work in the kitchen, "where they belong," so it really wasn't much of a victory for the feminists at all, since the "civil rights" victory against their "discrimination" is really just a big joke to the Bohos.

---

[13] *The New York Times* "Bohemian Club Ordered To Begin Hiring Women" (October 17th 1981)

The Unruh Civil Rights Act states, "All persons within the jurisdiction of [California] are free and equal, and no matter what their sex, race, color, religion, ancestry, national origin, or disability are entitled to the full and equal accommodations, advantages, facilities, privileges, or services in all business establishments of every kind whatsoever," so how is it that the Bohemian Grove is able to legally "discriminate" against women as *members*?

The Bohemian Grove, along with men's country clubs—or conversely, all-female organizations like the Girl Scouts, are able to turn down people of the opposite sex for membership without being sued for discrimination because these clubs are considered private, not public. Marcy Frost, an employment attorney at Moss & Barnett, explains, "If you are truly a private club, and not open to the public, the answer is generally, yes, you're allowed to discriminate on the theory we have a Constitutional right of freedom of association."[14]

It's called the "private club exemption" from civil rights legislation. This issue of "legal discrimination" gets into a gray area when people begin arguing over what is considered a private

---

[14] CBS WCCO-TV "Good Question: Why Can Some Clubs Discriminate?" by Jason DeRusha (August 20th 2012)

verses a public club. So, at least for now, *membership* at the Grove remains exclusively reserved for men, but they now have to include women (and teenage girls) as employees who serve the men.

Back in 2008 when Hillary Clinton was first running for president, Bill Clinton was speaking at a campaign event when a heckler began shouting at him about the Bohemian Grove. There was a pretty big crowd and security couldn't immediately make it to the man to throw him out and his repeated interruptions were derailing Bill's speech, finally causing him to respond.

"The Bohemian Club? Did you say the Bohemian Club? That's where all those rich Republicans go up and stand naked against redwood trees right? I've never been to the Bohemian Club, but you ought to go. It'd be good for you. You'd get some fresh air."[15]

His comment about "standing naked against redwood trees" refers to the common practice of members just whipping it out and peeing almost anywhere as if they were teenagers again at summer camp. It's a fun thing for them to do apparently, and is part of the Bohemian Grove

---

[15] YouTube "Bill Clinton gets asked about the Bohemian Grove club that he and other elites attend" (uploaded October 2011)

culture. The practice is literally encouraged and visitors have reported repeatedly seeing men everywhere around the club peeing on the side of trees or in some bushes instead of making their way to a bathroom.

Bill Clinton was also right about it being primarily a Republican club. Most, but not all of the members, tend to be Republicans who have historically been more involved with big business than Democrats. With the exception of Bill Clinton's surprising outburst about this "Republican club," no Democrats have dared to publicly denounce the Bohemian Grove, afraid of a backlash by their Establishment colleagues in Washington. Like the Bilderberg Group, it appears even mentioning the Bohemian Grove is off limits for most politicians.[16]

---

[16] See my book *The Bilderberg Group: Facts & Fiction* for a complete analysis of the annual Bilderberg meeting and the effects it has had on shaping the world.

Their Symbols, Saint, and Motto

The Owl

The Bohemian Grove's mascot (and logo) is an owl, or more specifically, the Owl of Minerva (or Athena, the Greek equivalent), who is the Goddess of wisdom. Interestingly this is the same symbol that Adam Weishaupt, founder of the Illuminati, used as his personal emblem as well.[17] Within the Bavarian Illuminati in Germany, Weishaupt had also created a level in the hierarchy called the Minervals.[18] An owl symbolizes wisdom because it can "see in the dark" which is analogous to being enlightened.

Pictures of owls are often seen in school classrooms standing on top of a small stack of books in order to symbolize knowledge. The National Press Club's logo contains an owl

---

[17] Barruel, Abbe- *Memoirs Illustrating the History of Jacobinism* page 582

[18] See my previous book *Inside the Illuminati: Evidence, Objectives, and Methods of Operation*, available in paperback from Amazon.com or e-book from all major e-books stores.

standing on a book for this reason. Owls are also seen as guardians, and you may often see an owl statue on the top of a building in order to scare away other birds in hopes of preventing them from congregating on the ledge of the roof so they won't dirty the building's face with their droppings—or worse, hit passersby on the sidewalk below.

The Dictionary of Symbols by J.E. Cirlot says, "In the Egyptian system of hieroglyphs, the owl symbolizes death, night, cold and passivity. It also pertains to the realm of the dead sun, that is, of the sun which has set below the horizon and which is crossing the lake or sea of darkness."[19]

A tiny owl can be found hidden in the design of the American one dollar bill, perched on the upper left corner of the frame that surrounds the "1" located in the upper right hand corner. This isn't just a case of people seeing something that looks like an owl popping out of a random pattern; it's clear someone purposefully included it in the design. Some people also see an owl figure designed into the street layout of Washington D.C., appearing on top of the U.S. Capitol building when looking at the location from overhead or on a map. This one is a bit more ambiguous, but still may have been included on

---

[19] Cirlot, J.E. -*Dictionary of Symbols* p. 236-237

purpose by the Freemason architects who are known for their use of occult symbols.[20]

There is also a giant 40-foot tall concrete statue of an owl standing inside the Bohemian Grove on the shore of their man-made lake which is the site of the Cremation of Care ritual. Many think the "owl" looks more like a demon with horns actually, and at its feet is a large altar where the life-size human effigy (called "Care") is "sacrificed" each year to kick-off the encampment.

Many people also believe this "idol" represents Molech, an ancient god from the Middle East that the Canaanite culture used to sacrifice their children to. Before the construction of the owl, there stood a large Buddha statue from 1892 to 1928 that was made of plaster of Paris. More on the Cremation of Care in a later chapter.

The Patron Saint

A patron saint is someone who embodies a group's philosophies or goals, and for the Bohemian Grove this is a man named Saint John of Nepomuk. He was a priest who received the confessionals of the queen of Bohemia in the 1300s, and when pressured by the king to reveal

---

[20] Ovason, David - *The Secret Architecture of our Nation's Capital* (2002 Harper Perennial)

her confessions after he suspected her of cheating on him, Saint John refused and was then killed by the king.

A large statue of Saint John carved from the trunk of a tree stands inside their forest showing him holding his index finger over his mouth, signifying the nonverbal gesture to keep your mouth shut and be quiet, paralleling Robert De Niro's motto in *Goodfellas* that you "never rat on your friends, and always keep your mouth shut." Their patron saint serves to remind Bohos of their oath of secrecy and that what happens in the Bohemian Grove, stays in the Bohemian Grove.

Weaving Spiders Come Not Here

The motto of the Bohemian Grove is "Weaving spiders come not here," which is said to mean that members and guests are not supposed to conduct business inside the Grove—"weaving" meaning working, but this explanation is just a cover story for the saying's true meaning. "Weaving spiders come not here" actually means "don't dare challenge the members," (or really, the "Gods," as they see themselves) and is an allegory that comes from an ancient story in Greek mythology.

According to the tale, a woman weaver named Arachne once disrespected Athena, the Goddess of weaving, by failing to acknowledge that her weaving talent was a gift from the Goddess and not derived from her own power. Arachne even pridefully boasted that she was a better weaver than the Goddess herself. Angered by her lack of respect, Athena then turned Arachne into a spider, subjecting her and her descendants to weave webs forever as a curse for disrespecting the Gods.

The Bohos claim that their saying "weaving spiders come not here" is taken from a Shakespeare play called *A Midsummer Night's Dream*, but given the elite's appreciation for the occult and Greek mythology, not to mention their elitist attitude that they are gods among men, this explanation appears to be simply just a cover story for non-members used as an attempt to defuse the allegations that they conduct business in the Grove, which as you will see later in this book is quite common.

Albert Pike, a favorite philosopher among elite Freemasons, wrote that "Masonry, like all the Religions, all the Mysteries, Hermeticism and Alchemy, *conceals* its secrets from all except the Adepts and Sages, or the Elect, and uses false explanations and misinterpretations of its symbols to mislead those who deserve only to be misled; to conceal the Truth, which it [the Mason] calls Light, from them, and to draw them away from it."[21]   So it should not come as a surprise to learn that the actual meaning of sayings and symbols by elitist organizations are not what we are told.

The Secret of Satan

When you first hear allegations about the ruling elite, or the Illuminati "worshiping Satan" it is hard for many to believe at first, but once you take a close look at the philosophies of the ruling class and the big secret of occult fraternities, it becomes undeniable that this is what's happening. Do you think this book just took a turn into "crazy tinfoil hat-wearing conspiracy land?"   Stick with me for a moment and let me explain and I'm sure you will soon agree.

Everyone, whether they believe it is literally true or just a myth, is familiar with the story of the Garden of Eden and the serpent temping Adam and Eve into eating the forbidden fruit, causing what is called the Fall of Man or the first sin. Adam and Eve were then banished from Paradise and the entire human race was cursed from that point on.

The big secret, or the "royal secret," as it is often called, is that many men (and women) involved in secret societies believe that Satan is

---

[21] Pike, Albert - *Morals and Dogma* page 104-105

not bad, but instead came to earth to free Mankind from enslavement at the hands of the Creator, who in their view is seen as a tyrant who wanted to keep humans ignorant, hence forbade them from eating from the Tree of Knowledge of Good and Evil.

The big secret taught within elite secret societies is that Satan the rebel "wanted to help" us poor humans, and risking his own eternal banishment from Heaven, he disobeyed God and encouraged Eve to eat the forbidden fruit to begin mankind's supposed evolution to Godhood by giving them the power [knowledge] that the Creator supposedly was holding back from them out of selfishness or malevolence.

According to the Bible, Satan claimed Man could "become like God" if they listened to him and disobeyed the Creator, and this is the secret of secrets (arcanum arcanorum) of the Illuminati. In 1854 French occultist Eliphas Levi wrote, "There is indeed a formidable secret, the revelation of which has once already transformed the world, as testified in Egyptian religious tradition…This secret constitutes the fatal Science of Good and Evil, and the consequence of its revelation is death."[22]

---

[22] Levi, Eliphas - *Transcendental Magic* pages 9-10

Manly P. Hall, who is considered to be Freemasonry's "greatest philosopher," revealed in his 1928 book *The Secret Teachings of All Ages* that, "The serpent is true to the principle of wisdom, for it tempts man to the knowledge of himself. Therefore the knowledge of self resulted from man's disobedience to the Demiurgus, Jehovah [God]."[23] Hall also stated that, "Both the sinking of Atlantis and the Biblical story of the 'fall of man' signify spiritual involution—a prerequisite to conscious evolution."[24]

Helena Blavatsky, who was a major spiritual inspiration for Adolf Hitler, wrote in her 1888 book *The Secret Doctrine*, that, "Thus Lucifer—the spirit of Intellectual Enlightenment and Freedom of Thought—is metaphorically the guiding beacon, which helps man to find his way through the rocks and sand banks of Life, for Lucifer is the Logos in his highest."[25]

Albert Pike, another highly esteemed historical figure of Freemasonry wrote, "Lucifer, the Light-bearer! Strange and mysterious name to give to the Spirit of Darkness! Lucifer, the Son of the

---

[23] Hall, Manly P. - *The Secret Teachings of All Ages* page 272

[24] Hall, Manly P. - *The Secret Teachings of All Ages* page 83

[25] Blavatsky, Helena - *The Secret Doctrine:* Volume II page 192

Morning! Is it he who bears the Light, and with its splendors intolerable, blinds feeble, sensual, or selfish souls? Doubt it not!"[26]

Even the infamous Satanist Aleister Crowley admitted this is what he believed was the biggest secret of life, saying, "This serpent, Satan, is not the enemy of Man, be He who made Gods of our race, knowing Good and Evil; He bade 'Know Thyself!' and taught Initiation. He is 'the Devil' of the book of Thoth, and His emblem is Baphomet, and Androgyne who is the hieroglyph of arcane perfection."[27]

Saul Alinsky, the leftist radical who Hillary Clinton wrote her college thesis on, acknowledged Satan in his book *Rules for Radicals* as the first rebel who stood up to the tyranny he said was imposed by God. According to the scriptures, Satan said, "ye shall be as gods," if you follow his advice, and this is what the elite are striving for. They believe that through this ancient secret and the emerging science of Transhumanism, that they themselves will "evolve" into Gods as the final phase of human evolution.[28]

---

[26] Pike, Albert - *Morals and Dogma* page 321

[27] Crowley, Aleister - *Magick: In Theory and Practice* page 193

[28] *TechnoCalyps - Part II - Preparing for the Singularity* (2008) Documentary by Frank Theys

The plan to "conquer death" is being promoted as a real possibility through Transhumanism, which involves modifying our DNA or all together replacing our biological brains and bodies with interchangeable mechanical and silicon based systems.[29]

This is a topic for a whole other book, which I am currently working on, but this is in short the top priority of the ruling class.   If my Transhumanism book is not out at the time you are reading this, there is a section on this topic in my book *Inside the Illuminati: Evidence, Objectives, and Methods of Operation* if you would like to learn some of the details about this disturbing agenda.

[29] *CNET* "Google exec: Humans will be hybrids by 2030" by Chris Matyszczyk (June 4th 2015)

The Different Subcamps

Inside the Bohemian Grove there are approximately 124 different groups or camps—each having their own sleeping quarters, kitchen and bar, and each managed by a camp captain who is responsible for overseeing their group.[30] Each different camp has its own unique name and consists of anywhere from a dozen to around one hundred men who tend to work in the same field to provide commonality and networking opportunities.

For example, the Hill Billies camp is made up mainly of men in big business, bankers, politicians, and media moguls from the state of Texas. The sign for the Hill Billies' camp, which the Bush family belongs to, consists of a cloven hoofed and horned Devil figure.[31] One of most elite camps is Mandalay, which is comprised of former presidents and other top political figures

---

[30] Phillips, Peter - *A Relative Advantage: Sociology of the San Francisco Bohemian Club. A Doctoral Dissertation* (1994) page 67

[31] Shown in Alex Jones' film *Dark Secrets: Inside Bohemian Grove* (2000)

along with major defense contractors. No seated president ever attends the summer encampment because his schedule and location is so closely monitored that his visitation would bring too much unwanted attention to the Grove, but once they are out of office (and before they are even elected) many make it a priority to be there.

Another elite camp of former presidents and high ranking military personnel and defense contractors is Owls Nest. The Hillside camp is made up of Joint Chiefs of Staff members and other top military brass. Other camp names include the Lost Angels which is where major bankers and media executives belong. Uplifters is made up of corporate executives and international business big wigs. The Rockefeller family and other big oil men have their own camp as well called the Stowaways.

It's quite obvious that having the Grove broken up into small subgroups which are comprised mainly of men who work in the same field facilitates discussions revolving around areas of overlapping interest. Sociologist Peter Phillips, who was a guest inside the Bohemian Grove on two occasions and who earned his Ph. D. by writing his doctoral dissertation on it in 1994, wrote, "Sharing a camp together at the Grove gives Bohemian directors of major U.S. policy councils ample opportunity to discuss current affairs and socio-economic policy issues. Watching and listening to reactions to Lakeside Chats by various other Bohemians also gives policy directors an opportunity to evaluate policy concerns from the broad sampling of the American corporate business community encamped at the Grove. In this sense, the Grove serves as an informal evaluatory feedback process to the top socio-economic domestic and foreign policy councils in the United States."[32]

Although the club claims the mid-summer encampment is just a vacation, and "weaving spiders come not here," some major world-changing programs have admittedly been hatched in the Grove. For example, the Manhattan Project (the plan for the atomic bomb) was admittedly conceived inside the club in 1942.[33] Aside from the birth of the atomic bomb, the United Nations was hatched from the inside the club as well.[34]

---

[32] Phillips, Peter - *A Relative Advantage: Sociology of the San Francisco Bohemian Club. A Doctoral Dissertation* (1994) page 127

[33] Phillips, Peter - *A Relative Advantage: Sociology of the San Francisco Bohemian Club. A Doctoral Dissertation* (1994) page 92

[34] Phillips, Peter - *A Relative Advantage: Sociology of the San Francisco Bohemian Club. A Doctoral Dissertation* (1994) page 93

Peter Phillips' dissertation reveals, "One of the foremost political events in which the Bohemian political network played a significant role was the United Nations Conference of International Organization (UNCIO), April 25th to June 26, 1945 in San Francisco. This was the original formation meeting for the United Nations, with delegates from fifty nations. Receptions for UNCIO delegates and key dignitaries were held at the Bohemian Club on May 17, May 29, June 4, and June 5. Towards the end of the U.N. conference the Club invited all delegates to a program at the Grove."[35]

It is rumored that Alan Greenspan was chosen to be the Chairman of the Federal Reserve Bank shortly after a meeting in the Grove where insiders came to a consensus that he should be their man. Arnold Schwarzenegger's successful bid for governor of California in 2003 after a special recall election to replace then-governor Gray Davis was allegedly given the green light by the Establishment following a visit to the Grove as well.[36]

---

[35] Phillips, Peter - *A Relative Advantage: Sociology of the San Francisco Bohemian Club. A Doctoral Dissertation* (1994) page 111

[36] *SFGate* "Behind the Count" (July 23rd 2003)

There is even a picture of Ronald Reagan when he was the Governor of California sitting down with Richard Nixon (who would be elected president the following year), taken in 1967 showing them inside the Bohemian Grove together where they were said to have been coordinating their future political careers.[37]   Nixon even admitted in his memoirs that the path to his presidency began with his visit to the Bohemian Grove.[38]

President Dwight Eisenhower's road to the White House also began in the Bohemian Grove. In 1950, two years before he was elected president, he was a guest during the summer encampment and gave a Lakeside Talk that impressed the Establishment insiders. We know of this because President Richard Nixon openly admitted it in his memoirs!

He wrote, "After Eisenhower's speech we went back to Cave Man Camp and sat around the campfire appraising it.   Everyone liked Eisenhower, but the feeling was that he had a long way to go before he would have the experience, the depth, and the understanding to be President.

---

[37] Phillips, Peter - *A Relative Advantage: Sociology of the San Francisco Bohemian Club. A Doctoral Dissertation* (1994) page 95

[38] Nixon, Richard -*RN: The Memoirs of Richard Nixon*

But it struck me forcibly that Eisenhower's personality and personal mystique had deeply impressed the skeptical and critical Cave Man audience."[39]   Nixon was later chosen as his vice president.

After learning how the geopolitical system really works once inside the Oval Office, apparently Eisenhower's conscience began bothering him.   During his famous presidential farewell address in 1961 when his two terms were up he warned Americans that, "In the councils of government, we must guard against the acquisition of unwarranted influence, whether sought or unsought, by the military-industrial complex. The potential for the disastrous rise of misplaced power exists and will persist."[40]

There are also rumors that in the build-up to the 2000 presidential election Bohemian Grove members George Bush Senior, Colin Powell, and other neocons had come to a consensus at the summer encampment that Dick Cheney should be George W. Bush's running mate as VP.

---

[39] Nixon, Richard -*RN: The Memoirs of Richard Nixon* pages 80-81

[40] President Dwight Eisenhower's Farewell Address in 1961

The Cremation of Care Ritual

When you learn the details of the Cremation of Care, or see the photos or the video footage, it becomes clear why the mainstream media has maintained a near complete blackout on this issue for decades. In the age of social media, word about the Bilderberg Group—which meets every spring in a five-star hotel for three days of secret off the record talks—has spread far and wide, so the mainstream media can no longer completely ignore their annual gathering.[41] While it may be somewhat simple to paint the Bilderberg Group as just another boring conference—explaining away the Cremation of Care is not so easy.

Basically, it is a human sacrifice ritual—only instead of sacrificing an actual person, they use a life-size effigy consisting of a metal skeletal framework wrapped with paper which is burned on an altar at the base of the 40-foot tall Owl Shrine. Close-up photos taken by a former employee reveal the effigy has two arms and two

---

[41] Checkout my book *The Bilderberg Group: Facts & Fiction* if you would like to learn more about this annual meeting of the ruling class.

legs and is the size of an adult. The ritual kicks off the two-week encampment at sunset on the second Saturday of July each year, where a small number of members carry out the ceremony while the majority of others sit on a set of bleachers and watch.

It is conducted by a "High Priest" who wears a silver robe with a red cape. He is accompanied on stage by around two dozen other men who wear long black and red robes, some of whom are holding flaming torches. The High Priest also wears a wireless microphone which broadcasts over a sound system so the audience of around 1000 men can hear him. He begins by saying, "The owl is in his leafy temple; let all within the Grove be reverent before him. Lift up your heads, O ye trees, and be ye lift up, ye ever-living spires. For behold, here is Bohemia's Shrine and holy are the pillars of this house. Weaving spiders, come not here!"

He continues, "Nay, thou mocking spirit, it is not all a dream. We know thou waitest for us when this our sylvan holiday shall end. And we shall meet and fight thee as of old, and some of us prevail against thee, and some thou shalt destroy...But this, too, we know: year after year, within this happy Grove, our fellowship has banned thee for a space, and thy malevolence that would pursue us here has lost its power beneath these friendly trees. So shall we burn thee once again this night and in the flames that eat thine effigy we'll read the sign: Midsummer set us free!"

It is a very elaborate ceremony with a live symphony orchestra playing music at certain points for dramatic effect. The effigy is called Care, and the ritual is said to symbolically be the killing of Care, or the ritualistic "casting off their cares" so the men can have a good time at their party. As the ritual reaches its climax and the effigy is set on fire, screaming is played over the sound system, and once it is fully engulfed in flames, fireworks are set off and the crowd cheers in excitement.

The High Priest continues "Oh owl! Prince of all mortal wisdom. Owl of Bohemia, we beseech thee, grant us thy council." A short song is then sung with lyrics that go: "No fire, no fire, no fire. Let it be kindled in the world where Care is nourished on the hates of men and drive him from this Grove. One flame alone must light this fire, one flame alone must light this fire. A pure, eternal flame, a pure, eternal flame. At last within the lamp of fellowship upon the altar of Bohemia."

The High Priest then concludes, "Oh, great owl of Bohemia! We thank thee for thy adoration! Be gone detested Care! Be gone! Once more, we banish thee! Be gone, dull Care! Fire shall have its will of thee! Be gone, dull Care and all the winds make merry with thy dust! Hail fellowship's eternal flame! Once again, midsummer sets us free!"

The first photo of the ceremony to be published came from a flier given to members within the Grove which was stolen by an employee and given to a group of activists called the Bohemian Grove Action Network which was formed in the 1980s by a woman named Mary Moore who lives nearby in the neighboring town of Occidental.

Radio host and founder of Infowars.com, Alex Jones, snuck into the Bohemian Grove in July of the year 2000, and using a small video camera secretly recorded the entire ceremony and released the footage as part of a documentary film called *Dark Secrets: Inside Bohemian Grove.* By this time, there had been various photos available online of the ritual and many rumors of its occurrence, but Jones' footage confirmed once and for all that such a thing did in fact take place. The footage can be viewed on YouTube and is quite shocking.[42]

---

[42] There are many different YouTube channels that have posted clips of Alex Jones' footage and his entire documentary, just search YouTube and you'll find them.

A British TV producer named Jon Ronson documented Alex Jones' infiltration for a segment of his own television series titled *Secret Rulers of the World*, which then featured some of Jones' footage. Ronson, initially a skeptic who appeared to mock the "conspiracy theories," was himself stunned to learn they were true. "As incredible as it sounds, it seems that some kind of bizarre secret ritual witnessed by world leaders really does take place in the forests of Northern California," he said.[43]

When Ronson contacted the Grove for a comment on the newly shot footage they gave him a brief statement saying, "The Cremation of Care is a musical and verse pageant heralding a two week midsummer escape from business cares and celebrating nature and good fellowship. As grand scale stage drama it may be a bit overdrawn, but it's about as innocent as anything could be."[44]

It's one thing to read about the ceremony, or see the photos, but the video leaves you with your head shaking. When I first saw it myself in the early 2000s, I thought it was a ceremony

---

[43] Jon Ronson's *Secret Rulers of the World: The Satanic Shadowy Elite?* episode 4 (at approximately the 32:13 mark)

[44] Statement from Bohemian Grove included in "*Secret Rulers of the World: The Satanic Shadowy Elite?* by Jon Ronson (2001)

conducted by a small and powerless pagan cult and that Alex Jones was crazy for claiming such high profile people were in attendance, but he was right. I first came across Jones' footage on a torrent site after searching for videos about the Illuminati. This was before video hosting sites like YouTube, Vimeo, and Dailymotion were created, and bit torrents were the primary way people shared videos through peer-to-peer file sharing applications like BearShare and Morpheus.

After Jones' infiltration, the club beefed up security and began using thermal imaging scanners and K-9 police tracker dogs to identify anyone lurking around the grounds who doesn't belong there. Anyone who attempts to sneak inside will be charged with trespassing.

In 2004, *National Geographic* magazine published a photo taken during a Cremation of Care ritual in 1915 and included a caption saying, "To purge himself of worldly concerns, a member of the elite Bohemian Club participated in a 1915 Cremation of Care ceremony—complete with candles and a robed and hooded comrade to guide him. This private club of influential men still meets annually north of San Francisco and uses this symbolic ritual to kick off its summer retreat. But today the ceremony involves burning a mummy-like effigy named Care at the foot of the group's mascot: a 40-foot-tall (12-meter-tall) concrete owl."[45]

Molech

In the ancient Middle East, the Canaanites and the Phoenicians would regularly sacrifice their children to a horned god called Molech (sometimes spelled Moloch or Molekh). This horrifying ritual consisted of building a fire at the base of the Molech idol, which had its arms extended out over the fire pit, and then having the village high priest lift up a couple's first-born infant son and place him into the arms of the beast, resulting in the child burning alive over the flames. Many people believe that this was the inspiration behind the Cremation of Care ritual.

David Icke, a popular British conspiracy theorist best known for his belief that the Illuminati are supposedly "reptilian shape-shifting aliens," claims, "Today, these elite names are still doing ritual sacrifices of children at Bohemian

---

[45] http://magma.nationalgeographic.com/ngm/bestvintage/photogallery_02.html

Grove."[46] Yes, David Icke believes the ritual is a *real* human sacrifice!

Icke also believes the earth is hollow with ancient civilizations living deep inside it,[47] and thinks the moon is a giant spacecraft just like the Death Star in *Star Wars* he says was built by aliens in order to watch over planet earth.[48]

The book of Leviticus in the Bible describes Molech sacrifices at length, and specifically denounces it as evil. "Don't sacrifice your children on the altar fires to the god Molech," it reads.[49] It goes on to give specific instructions as to the punishment for such actions. "The Lord spoke to Moses: You are to say to the Israelites, Any man from the Israelites or from the foreigners who reside in Israel who gives any of his children to Molech must be put to death; the people of the land must pelt him with stones."[50]

---

[46] David Icke in a lecture of his, shown in Jon Ronson's *Secret Rulers of the World: The Satanic Shadowy Elite?* Episode 4 (at approximately the 42:44 mark)

[47] Icke, David - *The Biggest Secret* page 250

[48] YouTube: David Icke - The TRUTH about the Moon - Interview with David Icke talking about this theory of his.

[49] The Bible: Book of Leviticus 18:21

[50] The Bible: Book of Leviticus 20:2

It continues, "I myself will set my face against that man and cut him off from the midst of his people, because he has given some of his children to Molech and thereby defiled my sanctuary and profaned my holy name."[51]

Music During Ceremony

The symphonic poem *The Isle of the Dead* by Russian composer Sergie Vasilyevich Rachmaninoff tells the tale of a ghostly ferryman who transports the dead in his small rowboat, as it moves slowly across the calm dark water. The symphony was inspired by Swiss artist Arnold Böcklin's famous *Isle of the Dead* painting which shows a coffin being transported to the symbolic grave depicted by the dark nothingness off in the distance.

Rachmaninoff's symphony is played by an actual live orchestra during the beginning of the Cremation of Care ritual as a hooded boatman dressed as Death paddles his rowboat along with the coffin containing Care across the pond in front of the stage where "Molech" stands. Beethoven's 7th Symphony is played later during the ritual.

---

[51] The Bible: Book of Leviticus 20:4

David Gergen Confrontation

A top advisor to Presidents Ford, Nixon, Reagan, and Clinton—named David Gergen, who also worked as a CNN contributor, was confronted on camera by Alex Jones on the streets of New York during the 2004 Republican National Convention where Jones walked up to him and asked if he'd ever seen the Cremation of Care ritual.

Gergen, looking visibly uncomfortable, responded, "Frankly I don't think that's something I need to talk to you about."[52]   When Jones asked him again about the ritual, Gergen snapped, "That's none of your damn business!" and walked away.   The clip can be seen on YouTube.   Why was he so defensive?   If it's just an innocent "play" then why not answer such a simple question?   Jones didn't accuse him of worshiping Satan or participating in an actual human sacrifice; he just asked him if he'd been there for the Cremation of Care.

Back in 1993 *The Washington Times* reported, "Presidential counselor David Gergen resigned yesterday from the all-male Bohemian Club, three

---

[52] YouTube: Alex Jones asks David Gergen about Bohemian Grove Rituals   https://www.youtube.com/watch?v=GHFoUZEjuNM

days after saying he would not run around naked at its annual Bohemian Grove encampment and insisting he would not quit [as the president's advisor]. White House spokeswoman Dee Dee Myers announced the resignation along with Mr. Gergen's departure from 17 other interest groups, charities and public boards ranging from the Trilateral Commission to the Very Special Arts Foundation."[53]

He also resigned from the Bilderberg Group, the Council on Foreign Relations, and nearly all organizations dedicated to setting up a New World Order, leading many to think that perhaps he grew a conscience and decided he wasn't going to have anything to do with such a plan any longer. Perhaps the reason he got so upset about Alex Jones' question was that he wanted to let sleeping dogs lie and being put on the spot about the Bohemian Grove freaked him out because he knows they cherish their oath of secrecy and didn't want to be seen as betraying them.

---

[53] *Washington Times* "Gergen quits Bohemian Club and 17 other organizations" by Frank J. Murray (June 11, 1993)

Walter Cronkite

Walter Cronkite was the anchor for the *CBS Evening News* from 1962 to 1981, and is widely believed to have recorded the voice for the Owl Shrine that is played over the loudspeakers during part of the Cremation of Care. This is especially interesting when you learn that while accepting the Norman Cousins Global Governance Award in 1999 at a World Federalist Association meeting, Cronkite made a disturbing joke about Satan running the New World Order and seriously suggested countries need to give up their sovereignty and yield their authority to a global government.

During this event Cronkite said, "What Alexander Hamilton wrote about the need for law among the thirteen states applies today to the approximately two hundred sovereignties in our global village, all of which are going to have to be convinced to give up some of that sovereignty to the better greater union, and it's not going to be easy."[54]

He then mentioned Pat Robertson's 1991 book, *The New World Order* and how Robertson

---

[54] YouTube: Walter Cronkite speech at the World Federalist Association receiving the Norman Cousins Global Governance Award

(creator of *The 700 Club*) wrote that the construction of the global government is the work of the Devil, at which point Cronkite added, "Well, join me, I'm glad to sit here at the right hand of Satan."[55]

---

[55] Ibid.

Author's Note: Please take a moment to rate and review this book on Amazon.com or wherever you purchased it from to let others know what you think. This also helps to offset the trolls who keep giving my books fake one-star reviews when they haven't even read them. Almost all of the one-star reviews on my books are from NON-verified purchases which is a clear indication they are fraudulent, hence me adding this note. These fraudulent ratings and reviews could also be part of a larger campaign trying to stop my message from spreading by attempting to tarnish my research through fake and defamatory reviews, so I really need your help to combat this as soon as possible. Thank you!

The Lakeside Talks

Every afternoon throughout the two week encampment a Lakeside Chat or Lakeside Talk is given just after lunch at 12:30pm, where a political insider or industry leader gives a thirty-minute speech on his area of expertise. These daily talks are a rare and uncensored look into the minds of the most powerful men in the world. The speeches primarily revolve around political, economic, and business trends, and often include information that is typically not revealed publicly.

A reporter named Philip Weiss working for *Spy Magazine* successfully snuck inside the Grove in 1989 and witnessed a Lakeside Talk given by General John Chain, who was the Commander of the Strategic Air Command.[56] In his speech the General lobbied the audience members to help him get the funding for the Stealth B-2 bomber program which would later end up costing almost 45 billion dollars, yes 45 *billion* dollars.[57]

---

[56] *Spy Magazine* "Masters of the Universe Go to Camp: Inside the Bohemian Grove" by Philip Weiss (November 1989) pages 59-79

[57] B-2 Bomber: Cost and Operational Issues (Letter Report, 08/14/97, GAO/NSIAD-97-181)

Every decade or so the club produces a limited number of yearbooks called the *Annals of the Bohemian Grove,* which are given out to members so they can reminisce about their time there. These rare books contain dozens of photos from inside the forest and some include attendees dressed in drag, along with pictures of the Cremation of Care ritual and various Lakeside Talk speakers.

I have personally been able to obtain four different copies of these books, (Volumes V, VII, VIII, and IX) since occasionally they'll find their way into used bookstores after older Bohemian Grove members die and their book collections are sold at estate sales or donated to thrift stores like Goodwill or the Salvation Army. In one book (volume VII 1987-1996) there is a clear photo of George Bush Senior and George W. Bush standing at the podium giving a Lakeside Talk in 1995 where Bush Senior reportedly told the audience that his son would make a great president one day.[58]

President Nixon revealed in his memoir (published in 1978) that his Lakeside Talk marked the beginning of his road to the White House, writing, "If I were to choose the speech that gave

---

[58] Rothkopf, David - *Superclass: The Global Power Elite and the World They are Making* page 284

me the most pleasure and satisfaction in my political career, it would be my Lakeside Speech at the Bohemian Grove in July 1967. Because this speech traditionally was off the record it received no publicity at the time. But in many important ways it marked the first milestone on my road to the presidency."[59]

While Nixon praised the Bohemian Grove in his memoir as the key to his path to the presidency, privately—as you will see in the next chapter—he denounced the widespread homosexuality he witnessed while he was there.[60]

Schedules of the Lakeside Talks are handed out to members inside which include who each afternoon's speaker is and what their topic is. Often one of these schedules have been stolen by an employee and made available on the Internet. In the next few pages you'll find a list of some of these speakers and their topics so you can get a feel for just how exclusive these talks are, and how the information presented impacts the world.

If the members' time spent inside the Bohemian Grove is "just a vacation," then why are there speeches by people like the director of the

---

[59] Nixon, Richard - *Memoirs* (1978)

[60] President Richard M. Nixon on the Watergate tapes in 1971 conversation with John D. Ehrlichman, and H. R. Haldeman made public in 1999 by the National Archives

Central Intelligence Agency, U.S. Army Generals, mainstream media executives, political analysts and talk show hosts, leading economists, and bigwig businessmen? The stolen program guides have revealed for example, in 1981 the Secretary of Defense Casper Weinberger gave a speech titled "Rearming America" where he urged his well-connected audience to pull some strings to increase military spending. In 1991 Dick Cheney, who was Secretary of Defense under George Bush Senior's presidency, gave a speech titled "Defense Problems of the 21st Century" where he did the same thing.

The Grove may have tightened up security in recent years, because the itineraries for the most recent years are unavailable. Some leaks did indicate who was speaking there, but the program guide of the complete speakers list and their topic is unavailable from 2012 to 2014. It is rumored that they may have stopped handing out the schedule to members since employees keep stealing them and leaking them to the public, and the club may be securing them under a sheet of glass so they may be viewed but not carried away.

In 2013 the local *Press Democrat* newspaper did report that four-star U.S. Army General Stanley McChrystal and comedian Conan O'Brien were among the speakers, as well as MSNBC's Chris Matthews, who also gave a Lakeside Talk back in 2003.[61]   There were rumors that Bill O'Reilly and Glenn Beck were there as guests or possibly speakers in 2013 because they were both missing from their usual schedules at some point in time while the encampment was in session.

---

[61] *The Press Democrat* "Retired Gen. Stanley McChrystal, Conan O'Brien highlight secretive Bohemian Grove gathering" by Guy Kovner (July 12th 2013)

Lakeside Talks 2011

Saturday, July 17
"The Supreme Court in the Age of Obama" by Jeffrey Toobin—legal analyst for CNN and The New Yorker.

Sunday, July 18
"The Obama Administration at War" by David Martin, national security correspondent for CBS News.

Wednesday, July 21
"How Should We Think about China. Partner, Competitor, Threat?" by Michail Armacost, former U.S. Ambassador to Japan and member of the National Security Council who handled East Asian and Chinese affairs.

Friday, July 23
"K—12 Education in America" by Joel Klein, Chancellor of the New York City Department of Education.

Saturday, July 24
"The Future of News" by Rupert Murdoch, CEO of News Corporation, the parent company of the Fox News Channel.

Sunday, July 25
"The Revenge of God: Religion & Violence in the Modern World" by Reza Aslan, professor at the University of California, Riverside.

Monday, July 26
"Venture Philanthropy—Andrew Carnegie 2.0" by John Wood, founder of Room to Read, a global non-profit organization that's focused on literacy and gender equality in education.

Tuesday, July 27
"Cultural Diplomacy" by Dr. Gary Smith, executive director of the American Academy in Berlin.

Wednesday, July 28
"Defeating IEDs as a Weapon of Strategic Influence by" Thomas Metz, Lt. General, U.S. Army (retired).

Thursday, July 29
"The Four Most Important Words in Economics: People Respond to Incentives" by economist Arthur Laffer.

Friday, July 30
"To Be Announced" by California Governor Arnold Schwarzenegger.

Saturday, July 31
"Why is Mars so Important?" by Michael Malin,
planetary geologist. Also "Countdown for
America" by David Gergen, former presidential
advisor.

Lakeside Talks 2006

Friday, July 14
"Global Financial Warriors" by John Taylor, professor of economics at Stanford University.

Monday, July 17
"Untold Tales from the Cold War" by Tom Reed, former Secretary of the Air Force.

Tuesday, July 18
"Energy, CO2 and Climate Change" by Lynn Orr, director of the Global Climate & Energy Project at Stanford University.

Wednesday, July 19
"Gulf Coast Erosion: Consequences for America" by Michail Armacosting, Chairman of Louisiana Governor's Coastal Restoration and Conservation Committee.

Friday, July 21
"America in the New World" by Fareed Zakaria, editor of Newsweek magazine and CNN host.

Tuesday, July 25

"Island Conservation with Guns, Traps & Poison" by Bernie Tershy, research biologist at the Institute of Marine Sciences at the University of California, Santa Cruz.

Wednesday, July 26

"The Parallelism & Ultimate Convergence of Science and Religion" by scientist Charles Townes.

Thursday, July 27

"Global Urbanization: a Challenge for the Future" by Richard Koshalek, President of the Art Center College of Design in Pasadena.

Friday, July 28

"Lessons Learned from War, Assassination, the White House and Hollywood" by Jack Valenti, former president of the Motion Picture Association of America (MPAA).

Saturday, July 29

"From Battlefields to Playing Fields: Economics, Energy, and Education" by General Colin Powell (retired), former Secretary of State.

Lakeside Talks 2005

Saturday, July 16

"Of Laughter & Leadership" by David Gergen, public policy professor and former presidential advisor.

Sunday, July 17

"To Be Announced" by naturalist Richard Leakey.

Monday, July 18

"The Case for Immigration Restriction" by Richard D. Lamb, professor at the University of Colorado and former Colorado Governor.

Tuesday, July 19

"Iraqi Medicine: Rip Van Winkle's Burden" by Bernard S. Alpert, M.D.

Wednesday, July 20

"Wealth, Poverty & the Threat to Global Security" by William W. Lewis, director emeritus at the McKinsey Global Institute.

Thursday, July 21

"Dark Energy & the Runaway Universe" by Alex Filippano, professor of astronomy at the University of Berkley, California.

Friday, July 22

"Unlimited Government" by Chris DeMuth, executive director of the American Enterprise Institute.

Saturday, July 23

"To Be Announced" (Name not printed, which usually means someone "important" who doesn't want to be connected to the Grove publicly).

Monday, July 25

"Nuclear Considerations: The Way Ahead" by Albert Konetzni, Vice Admiral, U.S. Navy.

Tuesday, July 26

"Peering Into Pandora's Box: Avian Flu & Beyond" by W. Ian Lipkin, M.D., scientific director at the Northeast Biodefense Center.

Friday, July 29

"To Be Announced" by Bill Richardson, Governor of New Mexico.

Saturday, July 30

"Hoover Talk" by General Colin Powell, U.S. Army General (retired) and former Secretary of State during the George W. Bush administration.

Lakeside Talks 2004

Friday, July 16
"Exploring Mars & Searching for Life in the Universe" by Charles Elachi, director of the Jet Propulsion Lab at the California Institute of Technology.

Saturday, July 17
"The Landscape of American Politics" by David Brooks, *New York Times* columnist and political commentator.

Sunday, July 18
"The Elections & Their Aftermath" by Norman Ornstein, political analyst at the American Enterprise Institute.

Monday, July 19
"State Building: What We Do and Don't Know about Creating Institutions in Developing Countries" by Francis Fukuyama, dean of advanced international studies at John Hopkins University.

Tuesday, July 20
"The Internal Life of Planets: A Comparison of Earth, Venus, Mars & the Moon" by Mark Richards, professor of geophysics and dean of

physical sciences at the University of California, Berkeley.

Thursday July 22

"The Coming Virtual Soldier" by Roger McCarthy, chairman & principal engineer at Exponent Inc.

Friday, July 23

"The Long War of the 21st Century" by James Woolsey, Former Director of the CIA.

Saturday, July 24

"The Unrealized Potential of the Technological Revolution" by James H. Billington, librarian at the Library of Congress.

Monday, July 26

"Remembering Reagan, One Insiders Account" by Kenneth Adelman, author and policy analyst.

Wednesday, July 28

"Did the Terrorists Expect the World Trade Towers to Fall?" by Ian Mackinlay, architect.

Saturday, July 31

"Politics, Plagues, Prevention & Preparedness" by Vice Admiral Richard Carmona M.D., United States Surgeon General

Lakeside Talks 1997

Friday, July 11
"Rogues, Terrorists and Two Weimars Redux: National Security in the Next Century" by James Woolsey, former Director of the CIA.

Saturday, July 12
"Augustine's Laws and the High Tech Grove" by Norman Augustine, chairman and CEO of Lockheed Martin Inc.

Sunday, July 13
Individualism in Western History" by Ken Jowitt , professor of political science at the University of California, Berkley.

Monday, July 14
"The Triumph of the Market and the Politics of Affluence" by Christopher DeMuth.

Wednesday, July 16
"Heretical Thoughts" by Yurek Martin, senior writer at the *Financial Times* of London.

Thursday, July 17
"The New Economics—Ideas Hatched in the Forest are Worth More Than the Trees" Craig McCaw, Chairman & CEO Eagle River LLC.

Friday, July 18

"Cyberspace and Managed Care: Is the Acceleration Manageable, or Do We Throw Momma from the Train?" by Louis W. Sullivan, M.D. Former Secretary Health & Human Services.

Saturday, July 19

"Plutonium Today and Tomorrow" by Charles Hollister.

Sunday, July 20

"National Security is Going South: Where is the Vision?" by William A. Owens, Admiral USN (retired) Former Vice-Chairman of Joint Chiefs of Staff, Vice Chairman SAIC.

Wednesday July 23

"Taxation with Representation" by Kurt Hauser

Thursday, July 24

"The Information Superhighway: A Way Upward, or a Toll Road to Nowhere?" by Ervin S. Duggan, President and CEO Public Broadcasting Service (PBS).

Friday, July 25

"Church, State and the Constitution" by Antonin Scalia, Justice on the Supreme Court.

Saturday, July 26

"Campaign Operative The Best of Times and the Worst of Times" Donald Rumsfeld, member of Nixon cabinet and future Secretary of Defense in the George W. Bush administration.

Infiltrations and Leaks

In 1980 a local resident named Mary Moore founded what she called the Bohemian Grove Action Network with the purpose of infiltrating the Grove by having people obtain summer jobs inside or by convincing those who already worked there to steal membership lists, program guides, and other information in order to expose the Grove.

Mary also organized demonstrations outside the Grove beginning in the 1980s consisting mainly of left-wing hippies who were concerned about the big business, environmentally unfriendly "Republicans" inside. She says, "When powerful people work together, they become even more powerful. The Grove membership is wealthy and becoming more so, while the middle class is steadily becoming poorer. This close-knit group determines whether prices rise or fall (by their control of the banking system, money supply, and markets), and they make money whichever way markets fluctuate."[62]

Due to all the attention the Bohemian Grove Action Network was generating, in 1982 a reporter from *Time* magazine decided to sneak inside but his story was censored by the magazine and never published.[63]

As I mentioned earlier, a reporter from *Spy Magazine* named Philip Weiss was able to sneak inside the club in 1989 and published an article titled "Masters of the Universe Go to Camp: Inside Bohemian Grove," detailing what he had witnessed. Aside from seeing a Lakeside Talk by General John Chain, who urged the audience to pull some strings to get the 45 billion dollars in funding for the B-2 bomber program, Weiss also said the members loved chewing on cigars, drinking beer, and peeing everywhere.

"You know you are inside the Bohemian Grove when you come down a trail in the woods and hear piano music from amid a group of tents and then round a bend to see a man with a beer in one hand and his penis in the other, urinating into

---

[62] *Sonoma Country Free Press* "Bohemian Grove Fact Sheet" http://www.sonomacountyfreepress.com/bohos/bohofact.html (now defunct)

[63] *FAIR.org* "Inside Bohemian Grove: The Story People Magazine Won't Let You Read" (November 1st 1991)

the bushes. This is the most gloried-in ritual of the encampment, the freedom of powerful men to pee wherever they like," he wrote.[64]

In 1991 a reporter for *People* magazine named Dirk Mathison was able to sneak inside and wander around for a period of time, but he was eventually spotted and removed from the property. He wrote a story about his experience that was supposed to appear in the August 5, 1991 issue of *People* magazine, but it never did. The managing editor at the time, Landon Jones, claimed killing the story had nothing to do with executives at Time Warner (*People* magazine's parent company) being members.[65]

Alex Jones from Infowars.com

In July of the year 2000, radio talk show host Alex Jones, founder of Infowars.com, successfully infiltrated the Bohemian Grove and actually videotaped the Cremation of Care ritual and got out with the footage. He cut a hole in the side of a

---

[64] *Spy Magazine* "Masters of the Universe Go to Camp: Inside the Bohemian Grove" by Philip Weiss (November 1989) pages 59-79

[65] *FAIR.org* "Inside Bohemian Grove: The Story People Magazine Won't Let You Read" (November 1st 1991)

shoulder bag and mounted a camcorder inside, and sat in the bleachers with the rest of the approximately 1500 members and guests and watched the event unfold. He was accompanied by his then-producer Mike Hanson.

A British journalist named Jon Ronson documented Jones' and Hanson's infiltration and included their adventure in an episode of his television series, *The Secret Rulers of the World* which follows Ronson as he "investigates" the claims of what he called "conspiracy theorists" surrounding the New World Order.

Ronson is a skeptic and appears to make fun of his subjects, seemingly intent to "debunk" their claims, but after Jones and Hanson emerged from the Bohemian Grove with the footage in hand, even Ronson was surprised that the "conspiracy theories" were true. After the two returned back to the hotel with the footage, Ronson questioned them about what they had seen.

[Ronson] Do you think this was unholy?

[Hanson] It's very strange to me. These people are supposed to be running the world and they're out there doing this.

[Ronson] You seem freaked out.

[Hanson] I am.

[Jones]   These people point their fingers all day and call people extremists or cult members or whatever for their religious beliefs, this was a pagan ceremony and engaging in human sacrifice, a mock human sacrifice…

[Ronson] Aren't they just saying that for two weeks they don't need to worry about anything?

[Jones] But they're burning someone in effigy and as it's burning they "ahh ohhh nooo!"

[Ronson] But they're not killing a person.

[Jones]   We understand they're not literally killing a person…

[Ronson]   They're killing something that is symbolic…

[Jones] Wait a minute. You saw it. You've got Death on this black boat bringing a pallet with the paper mache person obviously, it's got the feet and the head and they take it over and burn it.

[Ronson] But wasn't it just a metaphor?

[Hanson]   To me it doesn't matter.   I think they're sacrificing in the real world too.

[Ronson] Was this the New World Order?

[Hanson]   Yes definitely.   I looked the New World Order in the face out there.

Shortly after Alex Jones' posted the footage online, a show called *Washington Journal* on C-SPAN discussed his infiltration.   The show was hosted by Brian Lamb, the director of C-SPAN, who interviewed a "scholarly conspiracy researcher" named Michael Barkun who ridiculed Jones and appeared to be engaging in damage control.

The host states that he heard Alex Jones on *Coast to Coast AM* talking about his adventure and "he was talking about the Bohemian Grove club as if that's where it all happens. That's where all the decisions are made. There are thousands of people who go there, and there is some kind of ceremony and an owl and all that, have you followed this?" Lamb asked Barkun.[66]

Barkun replies, "Yes I have, even though the show is on past my bedtime, but, Alex Jones has

---

[66] *C-SPAN - Washington Journal* with guest Michael Barkun (March 12th 2004)

been talking about this for quite a while. The Bohemian Grove, of course, is a privately owned redwood grove, up in Sonoma Country, north of San Francisco, where every summer there is a get together of the wealthy and well placed, all male, who get together for general cavorting, socializing, lecture, symposium and so on, in an atmosphere that is completely removed from public scrutiny. Alex Jones and some others have suggested for a long time that there are all sorts of nefarious rituals that go on, and a matter of fact, and I talk about this incident actually in my book, someone who had listened to the Alex Jones show about this was arrested within the Bohemian Grove, very heavily armed, because he said he was trying to bring attention to what he thought were human sacrifices that were being committed by the elite who attend these gatherings."[67]

Barkun was referring to a man named Richard McCaslin who snuck onto the property in January of 2002 with the hopes of exposing the Cremation of Care ritual which he believed involved an actual human sacrifice. More on Richard McCaslin in a moment. Lamb and Barkun didn't even mention the Cremation of Care ritual, and how it clearly depicts a theatrical human sacrifice, and gave the audience the impression that crazy

---

[67] Ibid.

conspiracy theorists have just invented the idea out of thin air that the club is burning people alive during their party and the intruder was completely insane for thinking such a thing was happening.

The Phantom Patriot

In January 2002 a 37-year-old man named Richard McCaslin snuck into the Grove while wearing a superhero outfit, a bullet proof vest, and armed with a fully loaded MK-1 rifle-shotgun. Having heard the rumors about what allegedly goes on inside, and having seen Alex Jones' footage of the Cremation of Care, McCaslin was convinced there were actual human sacrifices being carried out and he intended to expose it.[68] Jones never said the ritual was an actual human sacrifice, but many people have, including, as I've mentioned earlier—David Icke, the guy who believes the Illuminati are blood-drinking shapeshifting reptilians from another galaxy.[69]

---

[68] *San Francisco Chronicle* "Masked man enters, attacks Bohemian Grove / 'Phantom' expected armed resistance" by Peter Fimrite (January 24th 2002)

[69] Jon Ronson's *Secret Rulers of the World: The Satanic Shadowy Elite?* Episode 4 (at approximately the 42:44 mark)

If you'll recall, the summer encampment begins the second weekend of July, and since "The Phantom Patriot," as he called himself, went there in January, not much was going on. After he didn't find any elite insiders gathering, McCaslin decided to set a building on fire and was apprehended by Bohemian Grove security. He was sentenced to eleven years in prison, a sentence dramatically increased because he was wearing a bullet proof vest in the commission of a crime (felony arson) which is an additional charge in California.[70]

Richard McCaslin was (and still is) part of the real-life super hero subculture, a small and bizarre group of adult males who like to dress up as "superheroes" and fantasize about being "real" crime fighters.[71] Some of these people actually walk the streets of cities in America wearing their costumes and see themselves as neighborhood watchmen.[72] After McCaslin was released from

---

[70] *San Francisco Chronicle* "Bohemian Grove commando found guilty" by Kelly St. John (April 17, 2002)

[71] Krulos, Tea - *Heroes in the Night: Inside the Real Life Superhero Movement* (October 2013) Chicago Review Press

[72] *Chicago Tribune* "Costume-clad activists hit Chicago streets to spread altruism" by Geoff Ziezuleqicz (January 18th 2014)

prison, he continued wearing his "Phantom Patriot" costume and still believes the Bohemian Grove members are reptilian shape-shifters from another planet.[73]

In 2011 he was seen protesting outside a business in Davenport, Iowa where President Obama was speaking and accused Obama, the Bush family, and Bill Clinton of being reptilians. A local paper did a story on him where he is quoted saying, "Every American president has British peerage [relation], and royalty has always said they have the right to rule by their bloodline. Their ancestors weren't human; they were aliens, probably of the reptilian type."[74]

Les Claypool, the singer of the rock band Primus, wrote a song titled "Phantom Patriot" for his solo project *Of Whales and Woe* (2006) which is about McCaslin's "raid" on the Bohemian Grove. Claypool lives in Occidental, California, a small town right next to the Grove and is obviously aware of the rumors and allegations surrounding the place. Here's a sample of the lyrics:

---

[73] *Quad City Times* "Alcoa protester believes Obama is an alien" by Rashah McChesney (June 29th 2011)

[74] Ibid.

Walking through the compound
With a formulated plan
There to help his fellow man
At this decisive point in time
The Bohemians of the Grove
Don't see it quite the same
Sensing danger in his game
They dub his quest a crime
- *Phantom Patriot*

Chris Jones

In the summer of 2005, a man in his late thirties named Chris Jones [no relation to Alex Jones] got a job at the Bohemian Grove for the sole purpose of infiltrating the club and gathering photos and video evidence of what happens inside. He was able to get photos of some of the camps and elaborate clubhouses, and even some close-up pictures of the site of the Cremation of Care ritual, including the effigy used during the ceremony.

His photos clearly show that the object burned on the altar is in fact a life-size human effigy. It consists of a metal skeleton that's wrapped with paper. Chris said he was able to inspect the effigy shortly before the Cremation of Care in 2005 and stuck his hand inside the paper wrapping to feel around inside it to see if by any chance there was an actual person, child, or vial of blood inside, but he said it was just paper wrapped around the metal skeletal frame.[75]   His photos and videos were included in Alex Jones' 2005 film *The Order of Death,* a sequel to *Dark Secrets: Inside Bohemian Grove* which first showed the footage Alex shot in July of 2000.

I have personally met Chris Jones and he showed me the photos and videos on his camera along with some other memorabilia he "kept" (stole) from the club, including a membership list, a program guide, a book of matches, and a trashcan.

When he first turned over his photos and footage to Alex Jones for publication on Infowars.com, Chris called himself "Kyle," wanting to remain anonymous, but after he was later jailed, he went public with his real name. Chris claims he showed some teenagers in his neighborhood the footage and photos he took, trying to educate them about the Bohemian Grove, but one of them got scared and told their parents Chris showed them a "snuff film" and says this was the start of his legal troubles.   He was later

---

[75] A personal interview I conduced with Chris Jones in 2006

arrested for lewd conduct with a minor for playing strip poker with some boys he was babysitting.[76]

Some people believe these charges were trumped up as payback for him working to expose the Bohemian Grove and for releasing his never before seen photos and video footage, but the court documents detail what appear to be a history of inappropriate behavior with teens in his neighborhood.[77] He claimed he was innocent and said the charges were based on misunderstandings but was found guilty in court and sentenced to three years in the Theo Lacy jail in Orange, California.

More Recent Attempts

In July of 2008 a *Vanity Fair* reporter named Alex Shoumatoff was arrested for trespassing after sneaking onto the property. Apparently he was working on a story—not about the strange rituals or the Lakeside Talks, no—he was working on a story about the club cutting down some Douglas-fir and diseased oak trees in order to help prevent

---

[76] 05HF1675 The People of the State of California plaintiff vs Christopher Jones 12/21/67 Defendant c6972092 http://www.fearnotlaw.com/wsnkb/articles/p_v_jones-33569.html

[77] Ibid.

forest fires—or at least that's what he said he was doing there.[78]

Shoumatoff later wrote an article in *Vanity Fair* titled "Bohemian Tragedy," where he complained about them cutting down some trees and talked about his arrest. He snuck inside, in his words, "to investigate reports that the Bohemians have been desecrating their own bower. That nothing is sacred with these guys anymore. Everything is fair game. But how could the Bohemian Club, where California's forest-preservation movement began, be logging its own land, which includes the largest stand of old-growth redwoods in Sonoma County?" he wrote.[79]

In January of 2011 the History Channel's *Decoded* included an episode about the Bohemian Grove and two of the show's "investigators" paddled down the Russian River in canoes and entered the forest from the riverbank which runs right along the edge of the Grove's property. They were discovered immediately and arrested for trespassing. This wasn't even during the summer encampment so they wouldn't have even found

---

[78] *San Francisco Sentinel* "Vanity Fair Editor Arrested at Bohemian Grove" by Pat Murphy (July 2008)

[79] *Vanity Fair* "Bohemian Tragedy" by Alex Shoumatoff (May 2009)

anything very interesting happening inside anyway.

The show didn't even include any of Alex Jones' footage of the Cremation of Care because the host, Brad Meltzer, said the History Channel's lawyers were afraid they would get sued for airing it since it was technically obtained illegally. At the end of the segment, the "investigators" talked about their experience and arrest. One of them said, "I had nine hours of incarceration to think about this. The more I thought about it, the less I was bothered by the Grove, even though they had just arrested me. I sort of felt like they are allowed to do this, it's their property, and if they want to continue to have presidents and Saudi princes and military leaders come here, they need to promise those guys that they'll be safe."[80]

Another of the "investigators" concluded, "There's nothing nefarious going on here. It's just a bunch of businessmen and a men's club."[81] Brad Meltzer the host ended the show by saying, "To be clear, this is a great club, and breaking laws isn't a way to get into it, but a bit more disclosure, a bit more transparency, would go a long way." Meltzer is also friends with President George Bush

---

[80] History Channel's *Decoded* (Season 1 Episode 7) Aired January 13th 2011

[81] Ibid.

Senior, who gave him the idea for the plot of his book *The Inner Circle*, which is about a secret society that's been operating in Washington D.C. ever since the United States was founded. This secret society isn't the Illuminati or any "evil" group with ill intentions—no—it turns out to be a "good" secret society that George Washington started, called the Culper Ring, which Meltzer's book claims is still in existence today to help "protect" America.

It's likely the *Decoded* "investigators" arrests were staged in order to send a warning to viewers not to attempt to sneak in. As someone who's been involved with a variety of "reality" television shows myself, I can tell you there's not much reality in them.[82] Scenes are staged and shot out of sequence to simplify the production schedule and then edited together to make it appear as if they were shot in chronological order.

In 2013 Colin Powell's personal email was hacked into by an anti-Illuminati hacker who called himself Guccifer. Powell's email inbox contained some photos of him and his buddies

---

[82] I was included in a different episode of *Brad Meltzer's Decoded*, as well as a variety of other shows, some of which were pilots that never got picked up. Check the "About the Author" section of this book for a more complete bio of the shows I've been involved with.

inside the Bohemian Grove, and one of the emails was from News Corp executive Andrew Knight asking Powell to "firmly point out" to British Prime Minister Tony Blair that he should attend the Grove's summer encampment that coming July and saying, "Tony has not yet got his priorities straight."[83]

Guccifer was apprehended the following year and sentenced to seven years in prison.[84] This is the same hacker who illegally accessed the emails of various Clinton, Bush, and Obama administration officials, including George W. Bush's sister's email where Guccifer found family photos as well as a self-portrait painted by George W. Bush depicting him taking a shower.[85]

On my YouTube channel there is a playlist of footage that I shot at the front gates of the Bohemian Grove in July of 2012 when I attended the Occupy Bohemian Grove protest, where hundreds of people gathered outside the entrance

[83] *RT* "Guccifer emails link Tony Blair to top-secret Bohemian Grove gathering" (March 25th 2013)

[84] *Herald Globe* "Guccifer indicted in US for Bush family email hack" (June 14th 2014)

[85] *The Washington Post* "Guccifer emails link Tony Blair to top-secret Bohemian Grove gathering" by Caitlin Dewey (January 22nd 2014)

to raise awareness about the club.[86] You can see dozens of police wearing riot gear standing guard in order to prevent the crowd from marching inside.   I also captured footage of a K-9 unit patrolling the perimeter of the property, a speech by anti-war activist Cindy Sheehan, and the rather violent arrest of one of the protesters.

---

[86] www.YouTube.com/MarkDice

Hookers and Homosexuality

San Francisco is basically the gay capital of America, and with the Bohemian Grove located just north of the city, one might expect some of this "gayness" would spread to the Grove, especially since it was founded by artists and "Bohemians." A Pulitzer Prize winning columnist for *The San Francisco Chronicle* named Herb Caen wrote about the homosexual activities in the Grove in his gossip column in the 1980s, and informants for the Bohemian Grove Action Network have claimed there has been widespread homosexual behavior inside.

Philip Weiss, who snuck inside in 1989 and wrote a lengthy article in *Spy Magazine,* said, "Today AIDS has put a damper on the Grove's River Road pickup scene, which Herb Caen used to write about in his *San Francisco Chronicle* gossip column. Just the same, a man on his own often gets invited back to camps by gay

Bohemians."[87]   Weiss went on to say that several men tried to pick him up during his visit there.

According to Mary Moore of the Bohemian Grove Action Network, a man named Don Heimforth, who worked inside the Grove, was the "Deep Throat" (referring to the famed White House informant during the Watergate scandal) of the Bohemian Grove in the 1980s, and claimed a lot of gay men were involved in the club. Heimforth himself was gay and later died of AIDS.[88]

In 2004 *The New York Post* reported that a gay porn star named "Chad Savage" was discovered working in the Bohemian Grove, supposedly as a "valet," which many people believe was just a cover story so he could engage in other kinds of activities— like perhaps "entertaining" the members.[89]   The Bohemian Grove yearbooks (the

---

[87] *Spy Magazine* "Masters of the Universe Go to Camp: Inside the Bohemian Grove" by Philip Weiss (November 1989) pages 59-79

[88] *Sonoma West Times & News* "Remember When: West County Community Protests" by Frank Robertson (November 22nd 2002)

[89]*New York Post* "Gay Porn Star Serves Moguls" by Richard Johnson with Paula Froelich and Chris Wilson (July 22, 2004)

Annals) have various pictures of men dressed in drag to entertain each other while inside, and one can only imagine what kind of weirdness goes on at some of the camps under the cover of darkness.

President Richard Nixon, who in his memoir admitted that the path to his presidency began in the Bohemian Grove, had something else to say about the place as well, which was not so favorable. In 1999 the National Archives released over 400 hours of Oval Office tapes from the 1970s, and on one of them Nixon made a pretty damning statement about the Bohemian Grove.

Nixon, along with John D. Ehrlichman and H. R. Haldeman, were discussing how the media was glorifying homosexuality and how it had been spreading, especially in San Francisco. Nixon went on to say, "The Bohemian Grove—which I attend, from time to time—it is the most faggy goddamned thing you could ever imagine, with that San Francisco crowd. I can't shake hands with anybody from San Francisco."[90]

---

[90] President Richard M. Nixon on the Watergate tapes in 1971 conversation with John D. Ehrlichman, and H. R. Haldeman made public in 1999 by the National Archives

Prostitution

It's common knowledge that many wealthy men like buying the pleasures prostitutes provide. Sex scandals and politicians go together like peanut butter and jelly and it seems a new one is uncovered every few months. The trophy wives of many wealthy businessmen and powerful politicians are often twenty or thirty years younger than their husbands, and many of these couples have an unspoken open relationship.

The wives sleep with the pool boy or men they meet at the gym, while their husbands buy prostitutes through elite escort services when they're away on business. And so, during the "greatest men's party on earth" at the Bohemian Grove, it would be foolish to think some of these wealthy and power-hungry men could spend a week away from their wives without buying some time with a lady of the night (or a call-boy).

The Northwood Lodge and Resort, which is just a few minutes away from the Bohemian Grove, is the spot where some men slip away to hook up with prostitutes throughout the two-week long encampment. Back in 2001 *Counter Punch*, an independent investigative news site, wrote, "A few years ago KGO radio, out of San Francisco, had an interesting talk show in which callers with first-hand Grove experience told their tales. A man from Monte Rio said he was only one of several towns-people renting cabins every year to prostitutes traveling from as far as Las Vegas to renew the Bohos' spiritual fibers."[91]

It has also been rumored that the Mitchell Brothers O'Farrell Theatre in the Tenderloin red-light district of San Francisco has been a source of strippers and high-class call girls used by the Bohos. Mike Hanson, who worked as Alex Jones' cameraman and producer, and who was with Jones when he snuck into the club in July of 2000, later interviewed four dancers from Mitchell Brothers for his book who claimed that prostitution was the "unofficial" but accepted policy at Bohemian Grove.[92]

These girls said that the strippers who had been brought inside to perform for the guys were always expect to "perform" in other ways, if you know what I mean. The girls Mike Hanson interviewed said they signed NDAs, non-disclosure agreements, preventing them from reveling information about their experiences inside, or even admitting publicly that they had

---

[91] *CounterPunch.org* "Meet the Secret Rulers of the World: The Truth about the Bohemian Grove" by Alexander Cockburn and Jeffrey St. Clair (June 19th 2001)

[92] Hanson, Mike – *Bohemian Grove: Cult of Conspiracy* page 192

been there, so they only spoke with him on the condition that he would not reveal their identities.

Hanson's book, titled *Bohemian Grove: Cult of Conspiracy,* details his and Jones' infiltration into the Grove, where he includes his interview with these strippers who were between the ages of twenty-one and twenty-five. They say they were hired for a three-day gig inside the Grove and on the first night they said they performed for a group of around 40 men and then later some of the guys paid the girls for their "company for the night."[93]

The second night they said they put on a show for a group of around 100 men, but the girls said they started getting extremely uncomfortable with how degrading some of the men were and got creeped out so they chose to leave before their third show and claimed the men wouldn't pay them since they had agreed to work for three nights and were breaking their contract.[94]

Hanson wrote that one stripper/hooker admitted she stole a laptop computer she saw laying around as compensation for not getting paid, and said that after she took it home and turned it on, she found pictures of what appeared

---

[93] Hanson, Mike – *Bohemian Grove: Cult of Conspiracy* page 194

[94] Ibid.

to be women and children being violently raped.[95]
More about these allegations in the next chapter.

---

[95] Hanson, Mike – *Bohemian Grove: Cult of Conspiracy* page 195

Allegations of Murder

In the past, when hardly anything was publicly known about the Bohemian Grove, rumors about the Cremation of Care "human sacrifice" ritual led many in the conspiracy community to believe the club was performing an actual human sacrifice every year.

After seeing the photographs and confirming that the world's richest and most powerful men do in fact meet in a secluded forest and perform what appears on the surface to look like a human sacrifice, it's understandable how many could come to this conclusion. But even though the details about the Cremation of Care eventually emerged showing it involves an effigy and not an actual person—accusations of murder still persist, and there are even allegations more disturbing than them supposedly "just" burning someone alive on an altar in a ritual sacrifice.

These allegations involve claims of horrific sadistic acts that are said to involve the sexual abuse of children and the production of snuff films (the videotaping of a murder for entertainment). These allegations are so grotesque and nauseating, I don't even like to talk about them, but I feel they must be addressed and investigated. I warn you, this section will be quite disturbing and graphic, and you may wish you had never read it.

These rumors, which I will detail in a moment, don't just lurk in the dark depths of the Internet, made by anonymous individuals on obscure websites or forums; but actually come primarily from a former U.S. Senator named John DeCamp. DeCamp was a Nebraska state senator in the 1990s who is also an attorney who represented several children who he claimed were sexually abused inside the Bohemian Grove in the 1980s at the hands of a pedophile ring allegedly operating within one of the camps.[96]

In 1992 he published a book titled *The Franklin Cover-Up*, where he claimed that a boy named Paul Bonacci was viciously sexually abused at the hands of a group of men inside the Bohemian Grove. DeCamp alleged the boy was forced to engage in necrophilia (sex with a dead body) and claimed to have witnessed these same men rape a young male child and then murder him during the summer of 1984, on or around July 26th inside the Grove.[97]

This was before anything about the Bohemian Grove had been posted on the Internet, and really before most people had ever heard of the Internet.

[96] DeCamp, John - *The Franklin Cover-Up* page 326

[97] DeCamp, John - *The Franklin Cover-Up* page 103

Paul Bonacci claimed this abuse occurred in a luxurious Northern California campground in an area that had big trees where men wore black hooded robes and where there was a giant moss-covered owl statue.[98] DeCamp says that when he asked Bonacci to guide him to the location of this alleged abuse, he said he led him to the gates of the Bohemian Grove.[99]

Paul Bonacci wrote in his journal about this alleged abuse right after it was said to have occurred. What he wrote is so horrifying I will not include some of it here because it will make you physically ill. He said that he and another boy he called Nicholas were forced to rape another kid who was then shot and killed immediately afterward, all while being videotaped.[100]

His journal reads, "After that the men grabbed Nicholas and drug him off screaming. They put me up against a tree and put a gun to my head but fired into the air. I heard another shot from somewhere and then saw the man who killed the boy drag him like a toy. Everything including when the men put the boy in the trunk was filmed. The men took me with them and we went up in a

---

[98] DeCamp, John - *The Franklin Cover-Up* pages 326-327

[99] DeCamp, John - *The Franklin Cover-Up* pages 326-327

[100] DeCamp, John - *The Franklin Cover-Up* page 104

plane. I saw the bag the boy was in. We went over a very thick brush area with a clearing in it. Over the clearing they dropped the boy. One said the men with the hoods would take care of the body for them."[101]

More details of Bonacci's journal are available in DeCamp's book *The Franklin Cover-Up*, and are far beyond the most gruesome and grotesque things one could imagine, and involve the alleged gang rape of a child and necrophilia.[102] In the first printing of his book in 1992 Senator DeCamp left out Bonacci's claims of the giant owl statue and men in hoods because at the time he thought it was too far-fetched for people to believe. DeCamp had never heard of the Bohemian Grove, the Cremation of Care, or the giant owl statue at the time. Only years later did he learn about the details of Bohemian Grove and became convinced that Paul Bonacci was abused there.[103]

When John DeCamp first told William Colby, head of the CIA, about his investigation, Colby reportedly told him to forget everything he knew and to, "Get as far away from this thing as you can. Forget you ever saw it or know it, heard it or

---

[101] DeCamp, John - *The Franklin Cover-Up* pages 326-327

[102] DeCamp, John - *The Franklin Cover-Up* pages 103-104

[103] DeCamp, John - *The Franklin Cover-Up* pages 326-327

anything else."[104] He said DeCamp was opening a can of worms containing forces too dark for him to handle. Only after saying he couldn't walk away from his investigation did Colby tell him he better get his story out before someone murdered him to stop it. Colby himself later died in what was called a canoeing accident, although many suspect he was murdered due to the strange circumstances surrounding his death.[105]

Now before you write John DeCamp off as mentally ill, or a conspiracy theorist, or perpetuating a hoax—you should know that around this same time the *Washington Times* ran a front page story with the headline, "Homosexual prostitution inquiry ensnares VIPs with Reagan, Bush," and detailed a shocking story of a gay prostitution ring operating in Washington D.C. that provided teen call-boys to some very powerful and well-connected men.[106] The man running the ring was a lobbyist named Craig Spence—who,

---

[104] *The Alex Jones Show* - "Alex Jones Interviews John DeCamp, Author of "The Franklin Cover-up" (July 21, 2004)

[105] *Pytha Press* "Who Murdered the CIA Chief?" by Zalin Grant

[106] *Washington Times* "Homosexual Prostitution Inquiry Ensnares VIPs with Reagan, Bush" by Paul Rodriguez and George Archibald (June 29th 1989)

through his connections—was able to bring several teenage boys who worked for him as prostitutes on a midnight tour of the White House, which was the focus of the *Washington Times* report.

The article begins, "A homosexual prostitution ring is under investigation by federal and District authorities and includes among its clients key officials of the Reagan and Bush administrations, military officers, congressional aides and U.S. and foreign businessmen with close social ties to Washington's political elite, documents obtained by *The Washington Times* reveal."[107]   The story quietly went away and has long been forgotten by most Americans.

A similar elite pedophile ring was also operating in London at this time (and likely still does today). *The Guardian* recently reported that major news agencies in England were gagged by the government in the 1980s to prevent them from reporting on powerful members of the British government who were suspected of being involved in an elite pedophile ring there which also murdered children for fun.[108]

---

[107] Ibid.

[108] *Guardian* "Media 'gagged over bid to report MP child sex cases'" by Daniel Boffey (November 22nd 2014)

The Guardian reported, "Two newspaper executives have told the *Observer* that their publications were issued with D-notices—warnings not to publish intelligence that might damage national security—when they sought to report on allegations of a powerful group of men engaging in child sex abuse in 1984. One executive said he had been accosted in his office by 15 uniformed and two non-uniformed police over a dossier on Westminster pedophiles passed to him by the former Labour cabinet minister Barbara Castle."[109]

The article continues, "The other said that his newspaper had received a D-notice [similar to a national security letter in America] when a reporter sought to write about a police investigation into Elm Guest House, in southwest London, where a group of high-profile pedophiles was said to have operated and may have killed a child."[110]

This is the London *Guardian*, not the *National Enquirer* or some random website on the Internet, and this story sounds exactly like the accusations Senator John DeCamp was making about a group operating within the United States at the same time, doesn't it? Two retired Scotland Yard

---

[109] Ibid.

[110] Ibid.

detectives recently came forward and said that a network of powerful and well-known politicians in the United Kingdom sexually abused and murdered young boys at parties but they were prevented from arresting them because they were part of what are called The Untouchables.[111] The detectives actually named names, including Cyril Smith, a popular member of the British Parliament who died in 2010, and who was a serial sex offender who preyed on young boys.[112]

In 2012 a paparazzi working for TMZ came across Ralph Rieckermann who played bass for the Scorpions, a popular rock band from the 1980s, and asked him if he would be going to any fetish parties while in Germany which are apparently very popular in Berlin. Rieckermann answered, "I don't go to fetish parties," but then went on to appear to insinuate that he had been to a "snuff party" one time where people were murdered for the partygoers entertainment. "I

---

[111] *Mirror* "Retired Scotland Yard detectives back up claims that paedo MPs murdered boys at sex orgies" By Keir Mudie, Mark Conrad (November 23rd 2014)

[112] *BBC* "Sir Cyril Smith: Former MP sexually abused boys, police say" (November 27th 2012)

went to one, one time—I seen some really bad shit," he says.[113]

When the TMZ cameraman asks, "Was it a donkey show?" Rieckermann responds "No, they actually, I think, it's...they actually killed people there and stuff. They pay up to $100,000 to see people get..." the cameraman completes his sentence, asking "executed?"

Rieckermann responds, "I'm not kidding. I went to another one where literally I saw like...the grossest...I wanted to throw up." The video, which can be seen on YouTube, then cuts back to the TMZ studio to show reactions from the staff. "He is dead serious. He's not laughing, there's not a smile on his face," one man comments. Another says, "I'm disgusted right now." Harvey Levin, the founder and managing editor of TMZ looked absolutely horrified, and said, "I'm shocked," and just shook his head.

Three years later, just days after I myself posted a YouTube video about this story, getting almost 10 times as many views as TMZ's original interview, Rieckermann posted a video statement on YouTube clarifying what he meant about the

----

[113] *TMZ* "Scorpions Bassist: Yeah, about those Snuff Parties I Went to..." (posed on the official TMZ YouTube channel on April 21st 2012) https://www.youtube.com/watch?v=1JiQAzZ0tzM

"snuff party." He said that he didn't personally witness anyone getting killed, but was at a party at someone's estate where the host showed him some of the bondage/sadomasochism fetish rooms where the owner said he and his friends would murder people for fun at special events.[114] Rieckermann emphasizes that he did not witness any murders but appeared to believe what the host told him was true.

It's not hard to believe that a group of extreme sadomasochists would find enjoyment by having someone murdered at one of their parties. The world's lust for realistic and brutal horror movies shows that millions of people find excitement in watching people getting tortured and murdered, and with films like *Faces of Death*, and certain websites which specialize in collecting gruesome photos and videos of crime scenes and people getting murdered, it's not that hard to believe that some people would pay money to witness an actual murder in person, or even participate in one themselves.

---

[114] YouTube: "Ralph Rieckermann official Statement about TMZ Snuff Party Video Clip" Posted on Ralph Riekermann's YouTube channel on June 4th 2015

Hunter S. Thompson

A man closely connected with what Senator John DeCamp called the Franklin Cover-Up (named after the Franklin Community Federal Credit Union in Omaha, Nebraska that was allegedly used to fund a pedophile ring used by high-level U.S. politicians in the late 1980s and early 1990s) has made some startling allegations about Hunter S. Thompson and the Bohemian Grove.

Rusty Nelson, [Russell E. Nelson] who worked as the personal photographer for the man at the center of the scandal, Larry (Lawrence E.) King, alleges that the famous "gonzo" journalist offered him $100,000 in 1988 to produce a snuff film involving the murder of a child.[115] Rusty said he turned the offer down.

Paul Bonacci also claimed, and wrote in his journal, that a man named "Hunter Thompson" was inside the Bohemian Grove at the time he was allegedly abused there, and also claimed that Thompson was the man videotaping his abuse.[116]

---

[115] Interview with Rusty Nelson on *A Closer Look* with Michael Corbin (April 12, 2005)

[116] DeCamp, John - *The Franklin Cover-Up: Child Abuse, Satanism, and Murder in Nebraska* page 105

Interestingly, Hunter S. Thompson wrote in his book *Fear and Loathing in Las Vegas* about receiving Adrenochrome from a Satanist, which is supposedly a powerful hallucinogen believed to come from the pineal gland immediately after a person is killed. Adding yet another twist to the story is the fact that Hunter S. Thompson wrote in his 2004 book titled *Hey Rube* about how organized pedophile rings keep children as sex slaves.

"The autumn months are never a calm time in America," he wrote. "There is always a rash of kidnapping and abductions of schoolchildren in the football months. Preteens of both sexes are traditionally seized and grabbed off the streets by gangs of organized perverts who traditionally give them as Christmas gifts to each other to be personal sex slaves and playthings."[117]

This writing clearly shows Thompson knew of the dark pedophile ring subculture. Thompson was known for getting personally involved in his stories, as was the case when he lived with the Hells Angels for nearly two years in the 1960s while he chronicled his activities for his book *Hells Angels: A Strange and Terrible Saga*. And so with Paul Bonacci's allegations that a "Hunter

---

[117] Thompson, Hunter S. - *Hey Rube*: First article titled *The New Dumb*

Thompson" was present during his abuse and videotaping it, and Rusty Nelson claiming Hunter S. Thompson propositioned him to shoot a snuff film, some are led to believe he was involved in even more sinister activities than hanging out with a motorcycle gang.

Hunter S. Thompson was a celebrity during his time and is still considered to be a counterculture antihero by many today. In 1988 during an appearance on *The Late Show* with David Letterman he appeared to have admitted to once being inside the Bohemian Grove. At the start of the bizarre interview Letterman asked him what he likes to do for fun, to which Thompson answered, "I like to kill."[118] The audience was noticeably uncomfortable, and the clip is available on YouTube—at least at the time I'm writing this.[119]

In his sometimes hard to understand mumbling Hunter went on to say that he liked the Jesuits because, "they're smart and mean," and that he himself had what he called a "neo-religious" world view. George Bush Senior came up during the interview since he was running for president at the time, and Thompson appeared to say, "I went

---

[118] *CBS* "Late Night with David Letterman" (1988) (at approximately the 7:12 mark in interview)

[119] YouTube: Hunter S. Thompson on David Letterman 1988 https://www.youtube.com/watch?v=B6JnkmFMhoU

to Hillbilly,"[120] which is the name of the Bush family's camp in the Bohemian Grove.

After his suicide in 2005, Thompson's former editorial assistant Nickole Brown posted an article online titled *In Memory of Hunter S. Thompson: Postcard from Louisville, Kentucky,* recounting some of the bizarre behavior she had witnessed while working for him over the years. "For weeks he played a tape recording of a jack rabbit screaming in a trap," she wrote. She also said that one time, "he threw me out of the house for refusing to watch a snuff film."[121] As she left, he allegedly called her a coward.

In an interview I conducted over the phone with Nickole Brown on May 20th 2005, she told me she thought he was possibly joking about owning a snuff film, and says she didn't think much of it after the incident, citing his "unique" character. She also said she couldn't imagine him being involved in anything like what Paul Bonacci and Rusty Nelson claimed. She believes Hunter was possibly investigating such claims, and may have pretended to be interested in shooting a snuff

---

[120] *CBS* "Late Night with David Letterman" (1988) (at approximately the 7:12 mark in the interview)

[121] Brown, Nickole - *In Memory of Hunter S. Thompson: Postcard from Louisville, Kentucky* (posted April 15th 2005) http://www.pw.org/mag/pc_thompson.htm

film as part of his own investigation into the rumors, which she thinks might be the source of these allegations.

Sex Magick

Sex magic is the belief and practice that through various sex acts, people can supposedly generate sexual energy and direct it to metaphysically shape the very fabric of reality. It's basically like mixing the visualization techniques found in teachings like the "Law of Attraction," popularized in 2006 by Rhonda Byrne's *The Secret,* with sex.

The Knights Templars, who reportedly learned about sex magic from the Tantrics of India, and medieval alchemist Paschal Beverly Randolph, and Satanist Aleister Crowley, all practiced secret sexual rites in what they considered to be the secret to "real" magic. Several fraternal organizations and secret societies such as the Ordo Templi Orientis, and the Chthonic Aurarian Temple also believe in—and continue to practice these kinds of rites.

On the surface, sex magic (often spelled with a "k" on the end, as stylized by Satanist Aleister Crowley) may seem like innocent sexual experimentation or a fun game, but the deeper one looks into the practice, the more bizarre it gets.

Multiple members and former members of the Ordo Templi Orientis, the secret society which uses Aleister Crowley's *Book of the Law* as their Bible, have admitted that the 11th degree of their hierarchy is dedicated to homosexual sex magick.[122] Former OTO member Jason Miller revealed in his book on sex magick, that, "the OTO's 11th degree is largely dedicated to the cultivation of sperm in the anus," and goes on to say that according to Crowley's diaries, "In some writings the point seems to be to cultivate the sperm alone, but in others it seems to be to combine it with blood that seeps in from tearing in the anus and remnants of feces. In this theory the blood attracts the demons and the sperm brings them to life."[123]

Miller goes on to say that a group of sex magic practitioners in Japan called the Tachikawa, supposedly engage in "skull fucking." Miller wrote, "One of the most infamous rituals they practiced is the empowerment of a human skull as a Honzon, a holy relic with supernatural powers... First the practitioner chooses a particular type of skull, such as the skull of a Shogun or an

---

[122] Kraig, Donald Michael - *Modern Sex Magick: Secrets of Esoteric Spirituality* page 62

[123] Miller, Jason - *Sex, Sorcery, and Spirt: The Secrets of Erotic Magic* page121

elder....He then has sex with the skull as well as with a woman. Then they wipe the combined sexual fluids on the skull."[124] Miller's book is not written to "expose" sex magic as sinister or evil, but instead to teach it, and he is an admirer and true believer of it.

The reason I'm talking about sex magic is because the group of men who allegedly abused Paul Bonacci in the Bohemian Grove were most likely doing so under the belief that they were engaging in some dark form of this kind of "magic." As a disclaimer I must mention that the Ordo Templi Orientis, along with former member Jason Miller, who I quoted above, do not advocate child abuse, pedophilia, or human sacrifice, but it's not hard to believe that some rogue members or a splinter group of a fraternity that practices esoteric sex magic have tried to follow in the footsteps of Aleister Crowley—dubbed "the wickedest man alive" in his day—by experimenting with, or incorporating child abuse and pedophilia into their rites.

Even consensual adult sex magic is strange, and the deeper one looks into it, the more disgusting the rituals become. One ritual involves taking a woman's menstrual blood and a man's semen and then mixing them together and baking

---

[124] Ibid.

the fluids into cookies or a cake and then eating it, believing that this gives people spiritual power.[125] Another involves placing sperm in the womb of a horse, which I can only assume mentally deranged people like Aleister Crowley have attempted through bestiality, which he is widely rumored to have committed in his quest to contact demons and gain spiritual energy.

With passages in Crowley's *Book of the Law* such as, "Worship me with fire & blood; worship me with swords and with spears, is the command...let blood flow to my name. Trample down the Heathen; be upon them, o warrior, I will give you of their flesh to eat! Sacrifice cattle, little and big, after a child,"[126] it's obvious he was a mentally deranged sadist.[127]

In some parts of Africa today, men believe that raping babies is actually a 'cure' for AIDS.[128] This belief is not as rare as you may think, and again, this is not something people just believed

---

[125] Kraig, Donald Michael - *Modern Sex Magick: Secrets of Esoteric Spirituality* page 56

[126] Crowley, Aleister – *The Book of The Law* page 40

[127] *Aleister Crowley: The Wickedest Man in the World* (2002) documentary film by Neil Rawles

[128] *Telegraph* "South African men rape babies as 'cure' for Aids" by Jane Flanagan (November 11th 2001)

500 years ago—it's what many believe *today!* Many men in Africa also believe that raping an albino woman is a cure for AIDS as well.[129] These beliefs and abuses are well documented by humanitarian groups and are not just an urban legend.[130]

With such bizarre, brutal, and disgusting "sex magic" beliefs out there, is it really that hard to believe that an inner circle of a secret society of power-hungry megalomaniacs would engage in rape, pedophilia or murder in hopes of gaining some kind of supernatural power?

Cathy O'Brien

In 1995 a woman named Cathy O'Brien published a book titled *Trance Formation of America* (a play on words for Transformation, using the word "Trance" to refer to a hypnotic trance) where she recounts what she claims is a true story of physical and sexual abuse at the hands of the CIA in their MK-ULTRA mind control program.

---

[129] *Reuters* "Albinos in Tanzania murdered or raped as AIDS 'cure'" by Fumbuka Ng'Wanakilala (May 5th 2011)

[130] Ibid.

In the book, and in her lectures which she gave at conspiracy conferences throughout the 1990s, she claims to have been taken to the Bohemian Grove where she says she worked as a sex slave for the enjoyment (and entrapment) of some of the members. "I was programmed and equipped to function in all rooms at Bohemian Grove in order to compromise specific government targets according to their personal perversions...I do not purport to understand the full function of this political cesspool playground as my perception was limited to my own realm of experience," she wrote.[131]

What she means is she allegedly was used to entice high level politicians into having sex with her while they were secretly videotaped for blackmail purposes, which seems pretty reasonable, but her claims soon get so strange, they are simply beyond belief. She wrote, "Slaves of advancing age or with failing programming were sacrificially murdered at random in the wooded grounds of Bohemian Grove, and I felt it was simply a matter of time before it would be me."[132] She went on to say, "Rituals were held at

---

[131] O'Brien, Cathy - *Trance Formation of America* page 169

[132] O'Brien, Cathy - *Trance Formation of America* page 170

114

a giant, concrete owl monument on the banks of the Russian River."[133]

It gets even stranger. She went on to claim, "The club offered a 'Necrophilia' theme room to its members,"[134] which she says included, "a triangular glass display centered in a main throughway where I was locked in with various trained animals, including snakes. Members walking by watched illicit sex acts of bestiality, women with women, mothers with daughters, kids with kids, and any other unlimited perverse visual display."[135]

She then says, "No memory of sexual abuse is as horrifying as the conversations overheard in the Underground pertaining to implementing the New World Order. I learned that perpetrators believed that controlling the masses through propaganda mind manipulation did not guarantee there would be a world left to dominate due to environmental and overpopulation problems. The solution being debated was not pollution/population control, but mass genocide of 'selected undesirables.'"[136]

---

[133] Ibid.

[134] O'Brien, Cathy - *Trance Formation of America* page 170

[135] O'Brien, Cathy - *Trance Formation of America* page 171

[136] Ibid.

So, in her mind, keeping child sex slaves isn't as bad as talking about their plans for a global government and world domination? The closer you look into the claims of Cathy O'Brien, the more holes you'll find. No Illuminati member or sadistic Satanist is going to be chatting with his friends about their plans for the New World Order in the middle of sex with a prostitute or sex slave! These conversations happen around a campfire, at lunch, or while sitting around having a few drinks in the casual atmosphere of the Grove.

And her claims that the Bohemian Grove has a huge glass display "centered in a main throughway" where children are abused and women are having sex with animals for the enjoyment of the members is absurd. In reality only a small fraction of the members could possibly be so evil as to enjoy such things and *zero* informants, guests, members or employees have *ever* mentioned such a thing. If such abuse does occur, it certainly wouldn't be put on display for the whole club to see and would be limited to a handful of individuals.

O'Brien claims that some of her abusers were George H.W. Bush, Ronald Reagan, Gerald Ford, Jimmy Carter, Dick Cheney, and Hillary Clinton, who she said performed oral sex on her on front of

116

Bill.[137]   Yet, for some reason after witnessing all this, her "CIA handlers" decided to let her live to tell about it?   Why wouldn't they have just killed her like she said they did to all the other supposed sex slaves kept in the Bohemian Grove?   Cathy O'Brien appears to be another opportunist who tried (and successfully did) make a bunch of money off the conspiracy community by claiming to be a first-hand witness to the activities inside the Bohemian Grove, as well as a victim of the CIA's mind control experiments.

Her book, *Trance Formation of America,* is written in the form a novel and includes long passages of dialog that O'Brien claims to have remembered after she was "deprogrammed" by a man named Mark Phillips who claims to be a former CIA operative who decided to rescue her.[138]   She claims that as a result of being subjected to the MK-ULTRA mind control program, one of her multiple personalities developed a photographic memory and could supposedly recall every conversation that had occurred in her presence.[139]

---

[137] O'Brien, Cathy - *Trance Formation of America* page 155

[138] O'Brien, Cathy - *Trance Formation of America* page 1

[139] O'Brien, Cathy - *Trance Formation of America* page 117

In case you're not aware, the CIA did conduct (and most likely still is conducting) horrific mind control and brainwashing experiments which began in the 1950s. Declassified documents reveal that these inhumane and illegal experiments involved sleep deprivation, drugging people with LSD and other mind-altering drugs, hypnotism, torture, and murder.[140] The existence of these declassified and confirmed experiments is what leads many people believe her claims since they do at least contain a *grain* of truth.

One of the goals of the MK-ULTRA program was to create mind controlled slaves or Manchurian Candidates, as they were called, who would willingly carry out any order given to them whether it included murdering someone, or putting themselves in harm's way.[141] Through post hypnotic suggestions these orders were designed to be forgotten after they were carried out. Several victims of these experiments have actually been awarded six-figure financial settlements for

---

[140] *The Guardian* "CIA sued over 1950s 'murder' of government scientist plied with LSD" by Karen McVeigh (November 28th 2012)

[141] Marks, John D. - *The Search for the Manchurian Candidate* 1991 Norton Paperback

the abuse they suffered, but Cathy O'Brien is not one of these people.[142]

She was most likely inspired by John DeCamp's book *The Franklin Cover-Up*, which first came out several years before she wrote her book,[143] where DeCamp, as I mentioned earlier, claims that numerous children have come forward saying they were sexually abused inside the Bohemian Grove and forced to participate in other sadistic acts.[144] John DeCamp's account of what he says happened to his clients is pretty straight forward, and as far-fetched as it may sound to some, the claims appear to be plausible and are centered around a small subgroup *within* the Bohemian Grove, not the entire club.

[142] *Chicago Tribune* "CIA Brainwashing Suit Settled" by Howard Witt (October 5th 1988)

[143] The first printing of *The Franklin Cover-Up* was in 1992, three years before Cathy O'Brien's book was released.

[144] DeCamp, John - *The Franklin Cover-Up* page 326-327

Author's Note: Please take a moment to rate and review this book on Amazon.com or wherever you purchased it from to let others know what you think. This also helps to offset the trolls who keep giving my books fake one-star reviews when they haven't even read them. Almost all of the one-star reviews on my books are from NON-verified purchases which is a clear indication they are fraudulent, hence me adding this note. These fraudulent ratings and reviews could also be part of a larger campaign trying to stop my message from spreading by attempting to tarnish my research through fake and defamatory reviews, so I really need your help to combat this as soon as possible. Thank you!

Talk Radio Hosts Dodge the Topic

Years ago when I first began investigating this subject, I thought I would test to see if the top call-in talk radio shows in America would dare address the Bohemian Grove, so I decided to start calling the shows trying to get on the air. I soon realized that every time I would get through to the call screener, they would hang up on me immediately as soon as I told them I had a question about Bohemian Grove. "We're not taking calls on that right now, sorry. Click."

I soon devised a method to actually get on the air and verbally confront the talk show hosts about this and other Illuminati issues. What I did was feed the call screener a fake question that pertained to one of the top stories of the day, and then they would place my call in the queue to be taken by the host. As soon as the host took the call—instead of asking the question the screener approved—I would fire off a question or comment about the Bohemian Grove.

I got recordings of many of these calls from the shows' podcasts and posted them on MarkDice.com and on YouTube to show people that hosts like Sean Hannity, Rush Limbaugh, Bill

O'Reilly, Glenn Beck, and others wouldn't dare inform their audience about the activities or allegations surrounding the Bohemian Grove.

Even with the seven-second delay, many times I was able to plant seeds in the minds of the audience before getting hung up on, and sometimes the hosts would argue with me for a few seconds before dropping my call and then telling the listeners I was crazy. On the next few pages are transcripts of just a few of these calls so you can see how they reacted to my questions. Sometimes I had to give the call screener a fake name like "John" because "Mark from San Diego" became a known problem for many of these shows when I repeatedly called into them week after week during my investigation.

First Call to Bill O'Reilly

[O'Reilly]
"Let's go to Mark in San Diego, what's going on Mark?"

[Me]
"Can you address the Bohemian Grove club private presidential…" [hung up on by Bill]

[O'Reilly]
"You know these guys in San Diego they're

just…the weather's just too nice there. Now here's what happens…not everybody…but you go out to the beach and you do all that…and some kind of substance gets in your mind. And Mark just demonstrated it." [referring to getting stoned]

Second Call to Bill O'Reilly

[O'Reilly]

"Ok, we've got an all-skate going on, which means you can ask me anything you want at 1-877-9 No Spin…let's go to Mark in San Diego, what's going on Mark?"

[Me]

"How do you feel about the private presidential resort the Bohemian Grove…" [Bill interrupts and drops the call]

[O'Reilly]

"I don't know what you're talking about, and I don't care."

This was on a Friday when Bill was having what he called an 'all-skate' in which he took call after call on any topic…or so he said. I could understand getting hung up on if my question was off topic, but this was the segment where O'Reilly said, "You can ask me whatever you want." This call and others can be heard on my YouTube channel, just look for the Bohemian Grove playlist on YouTube.com/MarkDice.[145] Bill O'Reilly quit his syndicated radio show in 2009 but continued to host the O'Reilly Factor on the Fox News Channel.

First Call to Sean Hannity

[Hannity]
   "Hello."

[Me]
   "The Bohemian Grove, have you been there, do you know about it…"

[Hannity]
   "I'm very aware of it, I've been invited, I've never gone."

[Me]
   "Do you know about the mock human sacrifice ritual, the Cremation…" [Hannity drops call]

[Hannity]
   "All right, goodbye. This guy's nuts."

---

[145] https://www.youtube.com/playlist?list=PLa8S4GilqogR8aZGfDIztCDZD_3ImeKHC

Second Call to Sean Hannity

[Hannity]

"Alright, back to our phones. San Diego, Mark on KFMB, how are you?"

[Me]

"Good. Let's talk about the Bohemian Grove and the kickoff of their summer festival in July which *is* a mock human sacrifice, Sean." [Hannity drops call]

[Hannity]

"You're out of your mind, you're a sicko...this guy's a nutcase."

Third Call into Sean Hannity's Show

[Hannity]

"KFMB San Diego, Mark next, Sean Hannity show, Mark, how are you?"

[Me]

"Let's discuss the issue instead of hurling insults and ad hominem attacks..."

[Hannity]

"You are a kook. You are a nut. You are absolutely out of your mind insane. I've never been to the Bohemian Grove, sir. It's just a great conspiracy."

[Me]

"You said you were invited, but have you looked up what happens in the Bohemian Grove?"

[Hannity starts playing the theme song from the film *Psycho* in the background]

[Hannity]

"I have no idea."

[Me]

"The Cremation of Care?"

[Hannity]

"No, I don't."

[Me]

"Look it up on any search engine Sean, ask your friends."

[Hannity]

(Sarcastically) "What do you think is happening in there?"

[Me]

"Well, they I think they're doing a mock human sacrifice where they burn an effigy of a human, it's like a paper-mache human body."

[Hannity]

"What Republicans do this, sir?"

[Me]

"Well, President Bush is on the membership list…"

[Hannity]

"President Bush? He's burning figures in effigies in the Bohemian Grove, sir?"

[Me]

"In front of Molech, the ancient Canaanite deity, while they're dressed up in black robes and colored robes carrying torches."

[Hannity]

(Sarcastically) "Yeah."

[Me]

"Look at Infowars.com."

[Hannity]
"Hey Mark…"

[Me]
"Look it up."

[Hannity]
"You are a nut."

[Me]
"Well, you're a gatekeeper, trying to avoid the truth."

[Hannity]
"You are a nut.   Go seek help.   Go get help." [Hannity drops call]

Call to Rush Limbaugh

When I asked Rush Limbaugh about the club, at first he pretended not to know anything about it, saying he had never been there, but when I pressed him, he made a fairly long sarcastic speech about the place, showing he knew exactly what it was and what goes on there.

[Rush]

"Mark, you're next on the EIB Network, hello."

[Me]

"Since I have you on the line, Rush, have you seen the video of the Bohemian Grove ceremony that Alex Jones produced that's on Google Video?" [the predecessor to YouTube]

[Rush]

"Uhh…No. Been invited to the Bohemian Grove, but I've never been there. And I've not seen the video."

[Me]

"Do you know about the activities within the Grove, can you talk about that?" [hangs up on me]

[Rush]

"No! Cuz I don't...I've never been there. All I know is that it's a bunch of elitists and power brokers who conduct secret meetings to take over the world and they run around nude. It's all men, no women are allowed. And they run around and you can find them going to the bathroom on trees and so forth. And they have men come out and make speeches to them and all that."

After his little sarcastic rant, he addresses his producer referring to my call, and says, "He believes it's the CFR in the woods," and then moves on as if nothing happened. The CFR (Council on Foreign Relations) is an elitist think tank that masquerades as if it were an ordinary committee in Congress that is composed of prominent politicians and journalists who are given policy recommendations and talking points which are practically viewed as marching orders by the Establishment. See my book *The Bilderberg Group: Facts & Fiction* to learn more about the CFR which functions as a less secretive sister organization to Bilderberg.

Call to Michael Savage

Michael Savage seemed skeptical and pretty shocked at first but did listen to me for a bit before he hung up with disgust after I asked him on air about the ritual for the first time.

[Savage]

"Mark in San Diego, you're on the Savage Nation."

[Me]

"Michael, why has information about the Bohemian Grove and George W. Bush's and Bush 41's membership been suppressed and ignored, and why is it laughed at in the mainstream media?"

[Savage]

"I don't know. What is so weird about the Bohemian Grove? It's a powerful group of men who have a club. I don't understand. What's the big secret up there?"

[Me]

"You haven't heard of, or seen the mock human sacrifice video?"

[Savage]

"Oh please. Come on. Do you have evidence of this? Is there any evidence you can post about this?"

[Me]

"Look it up on Google. Look at Alex Jones' Infowars" [website muted and not allowed on air].

[Savage]

"So everybody who goes to the Bohemian Grove including Henry Kissinger, is what, they're doing snuff movies up there now?"

[Me]

"Well, that's what senator John DeCamp alleges and his witness back in 1984, but…"

[Savage]

"Senator who? Senator who?"

[Me]

"Listen Michael, you really need to look into this, I'm surprised that you haven't." [Savage drops call]

[Savage]

"I have a migraine headache sir, there's only so much a man can do in one day. My God, now the Bohemian Grove, they're doing mock funerals. There's only so much madness a man can listen to until he goes crazy. You know, I'm serious. How much more can I take?"

Call to Glenn Beck

[Beck]

"Let's go to San Diego, welcome to the Glenn Beck program."

[Me]

"I was wondering if you've read the book *The Resistance Manifesto*. I know you're a big fan of the Bohemian Grove [sarcasm] and I thought you could expand on the rituals and the mock human sacrifice that goes on there each year."

[Beck]

"Yeah, do me a favor. Don't ever lie to my phone screener again. I'd answer that question if you would have asked my phone screener that question. Don't lie to my phone screener. We take you off the air immediately and won't deal with you. You might have just gotten that whole show that we were going to do on that topic taken out of line. I might not do it now because you pissed me off!"

First Call to Alan Colmes

[Colmes]
"Let's go to Mark in Oceanside, California. Hello."

[Me]
"Wondering if you checked out those photos or the video of the mock human sacrifice in the Bohemian Grove..." [Colmes drops call]

[Colmes]
"No I have not."

Second Call to Alan Colmes

[Colmes]
"Mark in San Marcos, California. Hello."

[Me]
"Hey, I was wondering since you've heard a little bit about it, and you've probably seen the photos and the video clips, I was thinking we could spend a few minutes talking about the Bohemian Grove and the mock human sacrifice that's done each year by the Republican elite."

[Colmes]
"What about it?"

[Me]
"What are your comments on that?"

[Colmes]
"I don't know much about it."

[Me]
"You haven't checked it out after hearing about this bizarre activity that the Republicans engage in?"

[Colmes]
"All right, thank you very much." [Drops call]

Third Call to Alan Colmes

[Colmes]
"The Friday night free for all is where you set the agenda, you run the show, you determine what we talk about, I do not. We take the calls in the order they arrive, and we cannot keep you off the air as much as we would like to in some cases, if you get through you get on. Mark in San Diego, hello."

[Me]

"Alan, if you type in Bohemian Grove into any search engine, the entire page is full of wonderful links and photos, and I'm sure that you've done this…" [Colmes cuts me off]

[Colmes]

"That's very nice. And I'm sure that someday you'll call me with actually a new topic rather than repeating yourself every single time you call me with the same thing. That will be nice."

Fourth Call to Alan Colmes

[Colmes]
"Hello."

[Me]

"Let's spend more than just a few seconds talking about such an important issue like the Bohemian Grove…" [Colmes drops call]

[Colmes]

"Well, first of all, you are a problem. You have continued since this show has been on the air to try to get to me to put you on the show as a guest. You're a phony and you're a fraud and I'm not going to put you on the air as a guest. Ok? It's not going to happen! That's that guy by the way, he has attempted to book himself as a guest on the show, he's left messages on my voicemail, has emailed me. We've talked to him off the air and tried to discern whether or not he was someone we wanted to put on as a guest. We decided not to. During the free for all, if he wants to call up and make his statements he's welcome to do it. That's why we do the free for all. And if we decide that someone is not someone we're not going to put on as a guest, I trust the determination of our producers, that's why they're hired to make those decisions."

The Belizean Grove

Apparently some wealthy and well-connected women were jealous of the all-male Bohemian Grove, so they started their own version for women—called the Belizean Grove. Not much is known about this girls' club, but there are a few pieces of information I have been able to put together. The Belizean Grove was started Super Bowl weekend in 2001 by Susan Stautberg who is the president of PartnerCom Corporation, a company which manages advisory boards around the world for businesses and governments.

In a response to her husband and most other men being preoccupied with the "big game," Stautberg gathered up a small group of her high-powered girlfriends and flew down to Central America for a women's weekend. This wasn't just a vacation; this was also a business trip where the women worked to further their careers and privately plotted their futures.

The group now consists of around 100 of the most influential women in the world who meet up every year in Belize for three days for what is said to be "a balance of fun, substantive programs, and bonding."[146]   The group says they are "a constellation of influential women who are key decision makers in the profit, nonprofit and social sectors; who build long-term, mutually beneficial relationships in order to both take charge of their own destinies and help others to do the same."[147]

One member, Mary Pearl, who works as the Dean of New York's Stony Brook University, said, "It's hard if you're someone who's a type 'A' personality, who's achieved a lot and who may be in the public eye—it's hard to make friends, so it's just a mutually supportive wonderful experience. We get together just for socializing and also just for intelligent conversation."[148]

It is bizarre that these women—most of whom are from the United States, would fly all the way down to Central America for a weekend getaway when they could just meet up locally at a fancy resort or one of their lavish private residences. Some speculate this is so the women can go out

---

[146] *New York Times* "Sotomayor Defends Ties to Association" by Savage, Charlie and Kirkpatrick, David D (June 15th 2009)

[147] *CNN.com* "Sotomayor resigns from women's club" (June 19th 2009)

[148] *Politico* "Sonia Sotomayor found friends in elite group" by Kenneth Vogel (June 4th 2009)

and have a night on the town with little chance of bumping into anyone they know or being recognized by someone. Perhaps it's like a Cougar's night out, when some of the women pickup younger men and bring them back to their hotel rooms, which if they did in an American city, they would run the risk of being spotted by someone who knew who they were, but when down in Central America, it is extremely unlikely anyone would recognize them.

Belizean Grove members include female executives from major banks, public relations firms, and even women in the U.S. Military. A *New York Times* article written in 2011 said, "Belizean Grove has connected the top women in technology to the top women in finance, to the top women in media, to the top women in law, to the top women in retail, and so on."[149] It is currently unknown if they engage in any occult rituals like their male counterpart at the Bohemian Grove.

The group was really only discovered in 2009 after Sonia Sotomayor was nominated for a position as a Supreme Court Justice by President Barack Obama. During the vetting process, Republicans digging for dirt on her discovered she was a member of this strange girls' group. She

---

[149] *The New York Times* "A Club for the Women Atop the Ladder" by Pamela Ryckman (April 2, 2011)

immediately resigned from the Grove since the American Bar Association forbids a judge from being a member of any organization that "discriminates" against anyone based on sex, race, religion, or national origin; and since it's an all-female club, this caused a potential hang-up for her getting approved to sit on the Supreme Court.

Founder Susan Stautberg was not happy about the new publicity, and said, "We like to be under the radar screen."[150]   In order to join, a woman must be recommended to the Belizean Grove "advisory board" which then decides whether or not to admit her. A few known members are U.S. Army General Ann E. Dunwoody; former Goldman Sachs executive Ann Kaplan; and General Services Administration Director Lurita Doan. Facebook's Chief Operating Officer Sheryl Sandberg, a major promotor of the feminist agenda, is a likely member as well.

Before taking over for David Letterman on *Late Night*, Stephen Colbert hosted the popular *Colbert Report* on Comedy Central from 2005 to 2014, where he pretended to be a radical right-wing conservative, basically satirizing Fox News' Bill O'Reilly. In 2009 when Sonia Sotomayor was being considered for a position on the

---

[150] *Politico* "Sonia Sotomayor found friends in elite group" by Kenneth Vogel (June 4th 2009)

Supreme Court, and the Belizean Grove was first discovered—Colbert joked about it in his monologue. "Now it has come to light that Sotomayor is a member of something called the Belizean Grove, a private organization whose members must be a female professional from the profit, nonprofit, and social sectors," he began.[151]

"This is not only more Sotomayor reverse discrimination—it also violates the code of conduct for federal judges which forbids membership in groups that practice invidious discrimination on the basis of sex," Colbert says, pretending to be outraged.

He goes on to say that Republicans have questioned her membership in this "sexist" club, and that, "There's only one way for Sotomayor to be a member of a single-sex club and still be confirmed for the Supreme Court, which brings us to Tonight's Word: Bohemian Grove! As opposed to the Belizean Grove, the Bohemian Grove or Bohemian Club is an all-male, 130-year-old secret society of captains of industry, international power brokers and every Republican president since 1923. Herbert Hoover called it quote 'the greatest men's party on earth,' and Richard Nixon agreed,"

---

[151] *Comedy Central* - "The Colbert Report" (June 17th 2009) http://thecolbertreport.cc.com/videos/v8qfms/the-word---bohemian-grove

he says sarcastically before playing the White House Oval Office tape of Nixon calling it the most faggy God damned thing you could ever imagine.[152] "That is really saying something from a guy named tricky dick," Colbert continues.

"Every year, the Bohemian Club holds a retreat in the Bohemian Grove in northern California where they are rumored to engage in costumed pageantry, simulated human sacrifice and worshiping before a 40-foot stone owl. In 1999 after being denied membership in the Bohemian Grove, a group of women started their own same sex organization—the Belizean Grove."

He then quotes a statement from Sotomayor denying they discriminate against men, reading "All interested individuals are duly considered by the membership committee [and] to the best of my knowledge, a man has never asked to be considered for membership."

"Until now!" Colbert says. "Because I hereby demand to be admitted to this ladies' shadowy cabal. Making me a member is the quickest way to put this controversy to rest...and between you and me, the Bohemian Grove is a total sausage fest. I can't spend another summer watching Henry Kissinger belly dance around a statue of the

---

[152] President Richard M. Nixon on the Watergate tapes in 1971 conversation with John D. Ehrlichman, and H. R. Haldeman made public in 1999 by the National Archives

tootsie pop owl, so madam I await your invitation."

Depictions in Television and Film

Eyes Wide Shut

In 1999 Tom Cruise and his then-wife Nicole Kidman stared in *Eyes Wide Shut*, a bizarre film directed by Stanley Kubrick about a secret society of wealthy men and women in New York City who meet periodically in large mansions to engage in strange ceremonies and masked sex orgies.

Tom Cruise's character (Dr. Bill Hartford) is told about the parties by a friend of his who is paid to play the piano during the events. Out of curiosity Cruise rents a black robe and a mask from a local costume shop, and attends one of the parties. Once inside he witnesses a group of around 100 men and women conducting some kind of occult ritual while wearing long black robes and venetian masks just before having an orgy.

Tom Cruise is eventually discovered and escorted from the property after being given an ominous threat to remain silent about what he had seen. The following day, one of his wealthy friends reveals that he was in attendance at the ceremonial orgy and warned Cruise, "Do you have any idea how much trouble you got yourself into last night just by going over there? Who do you think those people were? Those were not just some ordinary people. If I told you their names...no, I'm not going to tell you their names...but if I did, I don't think you'd sleep so well at night."

As strange as it sounds, the plot of *Eyes Wide Shut* is based on actual events, and for some, the film brought to mind images of the Bohemian Grove or the rumored Illuminati sex orgies many believe occur at the private parties of the ruling elite. The Hellfire Club was a sex club in England where members of Europe's class would have sex orgies back in the eighteenth century.[153]

The club's name was a celebration of the Hellfire that sin is said to bring, and their motto was "Do what thou wilt," the same credo Aleister Crowley would adopt over 100 years later. The Hellfire club was a place where European royalty and wealthy men would get drunk and have group sex with prostitutes or loose women from their social circles. But sex clubs and swinger parties

---

[153] *The Irish Times* "Uncovering the origins of Dublin's Hellfire Club" by David Ryan (August 10th 2012)

aren't just a thing of the past. In fact, today, they are more popular than ever.

In recent years a franchise of secretive elite sex clubs called Killing Kittens has popped up in Europe and the United States that hold *Eyes Wide Shut* themed parties in rented mansions in major cities like London, Los Angeles, and New York. Couples pay $250 per party to participate in masked orgies with other strangers.[154] The Killing Kittens club vets all requests and couples must be approved before they are allowed to attend a "Kittens Party."[155] Everyone wears a venetian mask, just like the party in *Eyes Wide Shut,* and everyone has sex with whoever they want, wherever they want, throughout the mansion right in front of everyone else.

A Christian singer named Jeannie Ortega, who had one of her singles reach the Billboard Top 100, wrote a blog in February of 2015 talking about how a record producer she once worked with said he was invited to an *Eyes Wide Shut*-type of party that was allegedly thrown by rapper Jay Z. "I was working with him [the producer] on my

---

[154] *New York Post* "Kate Middleton's pal hosts the swankiest sex party in NYC" by Dana Schuster (March 10th 2015)

[155] *New York Post* "A night inside the sex club hosted by Kate Middleton's pal" by Dana Schuster (March 17th 2015

album and we had a conversation about the abnormal things the entertainment industry is involved in. At the time the word 'Illuminati' was not as popular, so we called it more so Freemasonry or something like that. The producer proceeded to share with me his own experiences while on Roc-A Fella while Jay-Z was a part of the company. He said he was once invited to a party where he was given a poker chip and asked to go to the party wearing a black trench coat with nothing else underneath it." [156]

The poker chip was supposedly the entrance pass. The producer, who Ortega did not name, said he did not attend. It's standard operation procedure to have people sign non-disclosure agreements when attending elite parties so they are legally prevented from talking about them and strict security measures are put in place which enforce a no cell phone policy so no pictures can be taken inside. Are such sex parties thrown by the Hollywood and political elite today like they were in the days of the Hellfire club?

Billionaire Jeffrey Epstein—a personal friend of Bill Clinton—who also rubs elbows with many

---

[156] *BreathCast* "Questlove Recounts Illuminati Experience with Jay-Z? Christian Artist Shares Own Experience with the Occult in Music Industry" by Jeannie Ortega (February 17th 2015)

political and Hollywood elite, is accused of organizing orgies with underage prostitutes and sex slaves to entertain him and his friends on his luxurious and secluded Virgin Islands estate.[157] Epstein is a sex offender, having been convicted of soliciting underage prostitutes in the past as young as fourteen-years-old.[158]   Court documents also claim that Epstein had the bedrooms in his estate fitted with hidden cameras to videotape his high-powered guests' encounters with prostitutes so he could allegedly then use the videos to blackmail them.[159]

With swinger clubs becoming more and more popular, and websites and apps like Adult Friend Finder, a place where couples go to meet other couples and fulfill their strange sexual fetishes— and the well-known sexual deviancy of many powerful politicians and Hollywood elite, it

---

[157] *Newsweek* "Jeffrey Epstein: The Sex Offender Who Mixes With Princes and Premiers" by Catherine Ostler (January 29th 2015)

[158] *The Guardian* "Jeffrey Epstein's donations to young pupils prompts US Virgin Islands review" by Jon Swaine (January 13th 2015)

[159] *The Mirror* "Prince Andrew may have been secretly filmed with underage girl he is alleged to have abused" by Matthew Drake (January 3, 3015)

shouldn't be much of a surprise that *Eyes Wide Shut* parties occur. It's likely that at some point in the future these sex magic orgy practitioners will come out of the closet and demand that the world accept their activities as "normal," much in the same way we saw the gay rights movement grow from a ripple to a tidal wave in the early 21st century.

South Park

Known for its no holds barred lampooning of pop culture figures, politicians, and religious beliefs, *South Park* tries to be as offensive as possible with their crude and often distasteful "humor." Occasionally the show ridicules various people and institutions by simply presenting bizarre facts in a humorous way, like they did in their episodes making fun of Mormonism and Scientology. Both of these episodes included a banner on the bottom of the screen that read, "This is actually what Mormons/Scientologists believe," and it really was what they believe! This disclaimer was used to point out the fact that the show wasn't making up these foolish beliefs, which made the episodes even more hilarious.

The use of this banner was also included in an episode about what was called the "Super Adventure Club." This episode, titled "The

Return of Chef," was about an organization of pedophiles who travel around the world to have sex with young boys because they believe that it gives them magical powers. The current leader of the group explains, "Our club offers hope. Do you think we go around the world molesting children because it feels really good? No. Our club has a message and a secret that explains the mysteries of life."[160]

The leader continues to explain the history of the "Super Adventure Club," saying that a man named William P. Phineas, a pedophile who traveled all over the world molesting young boys, discovered a great secret. "But now the most wonderful part. You see, after having sex with all those children, Phineas realized that molesting all those kids had made him immortal. He discovered that children have things called marlocks in their bodies and when an adult has sex with a child, the marlocks implode feeding the adult's receptor cavity with energy that causes immortality."[161]

While this is not funny at all, and only in a morally bankrupt society would such dialogue be allowed to air on a major network like Comedy Central, the plot appears to have been inspired by

---

[160] Comedy Central - *South Park* "The Return of Chef" Season 10 Episode 1 (March 22nd 2006)

[161] Ibid.

the teachings of satanic sex magic—which—as I covered earlier in this book, is the belief that certain perverted sexual practices unlock spiritual powers latent in the mind. As I pointed out, Satanist Aleister Crowley believed that though sex magic a person could summon demons that would grant them supernatural power, and some believe that if these rituals involve children, it will enable them to harness "real" black magic forces.

South Park's creators and writers Trey Parker and Matt Stone must have stumbled across this idea since there are probably whispers in Hollywood about people doing such things. Aleister Crowley is highly revered by many musicians and celebrities today.[162] And again, just like the episodes making fun of Mormonism and Scientology, this episode included the note on the bottom of the screen saying, "This is what the Super Adventure Club actually believes."

How could the writers have possibly come up with such a crazy idea out of the blue, and why would they put a banner at the bottom of the screen saying this is what these people actually believe in the same manner they did in the other episodes about strange religious beliefs if they weren't in a sense trying to be serious?

---

[162] See my previous book *Illuminati in the Music Industry.*

The "Super Adventure Club" is possibly a reference to NAMBLA, the North American Man Boy Love Association, a "pedophile rights" group which claims there is nothing wrong with pedophilia, and want society to accept it as "normal" as many have in the case of homosexuality. It wouldn't be surprising at all to learn that NAMBLA members had incorporated satanic sex magic into their teachings as another way to try to justify their mental illness and child abuse.

Teddy Bears' Picnic

The man who did the voice for Mr. Burns on *The Simpsons* for over twenty-five years, Harry Shearer, wrote and directed a little known (and commercial failure) which was a spoof on the Bohemian Grove. *Teddy Bears' Picnic* went straight to DVD and was too terrible for any distributer to put it in theaters. The movie was made in 2002; just two years after Alex Jones had infiltrated the Bohemian Grove and videotaped the Cremation of Care ritual, which served as Shearer's inspiration for his film.

The plot of *Teddy Bears' Picnic* involves an exclusive men's club called Zambezi Glen that meets in the woods for their annual summer party where they get drunk, dress in drag, enjoy peeing on trees, and have sex with prostitutes. An employee of the campground secretly videotapes some of the members' activities hoping to sell the footage to the media, but is spotted and chased into the woods. The well-connected men of Zambezi Glen then call in the military to track the guy down using helicopters and K-9s, and in the process end up accidentally setting the forest on fire.

The Molech statue in the Grove is depicted as a large pelican in Shearer's film, and club members dress up in Halloween-type witch costumes and conduct a ritual called the "Assassination of Time." Shearer has admitted to being a guest at the Bohemian Grove and talked about his experience there with British television producer Jon Ronson in an episode of his *Secret Rulers of the World* series which basically makes fun of New World Order conspiracy theorists.

Being a left-wing Hollywood liberal, Shearer labeled the members of Bohemian Grove "white Christians." He told Ronson, "You don't have to be a conspiracy theorist to know that this is a get together of very powerful guys. Whatever it is they're doing there, whether they're running the world or just reliving their adolescence, they're a self-selected group of powerful white Christian Americans."[163]

He then went on to say he likes conspiracy theories because he thinks they're entertaining, but doesn't believe they are true. "I love the theories, because I believe that these people are the only real good narrative writers left in the English language. They do write really good compelling narratives, but I just don't happen to think they're true."

In the interview he then goes on to stereotype conspiracy theorists as gun-loving, backwoods hicks who live in the middle of nowhere. "And you can imagine, I'm in New York and they're keeping me spellbound. Imagine being isolated on a ranch in Montana with nobody except your son, who you're teaching to shoot a rifle, this would be some amazing stuff coming through the night to you, you know."[164] Apparently Harry Shearer thinks Montana is stuck back in the 1800s.

Ronson asked him if he thought the Bohemian Grove was a secret society, to which Shearer answered, "Yeah but I mean it's a secret society the way the secret society that I was inducted into at UCLA in my senior year is a secret society.

---

[163] Jon Ronson's *Secret Rulers of the World: The Satanic Shadowy Elite?* Episode 4 (at approximately the 42:12 mark)

[164] Ibid.

There is a lot of meaningless mumbo jumbo and the main conspiracy is to take it seriously."

"If you've ever been through a secret society in college, you know this stuff. Just add two zeros to the budget and you're doing what you did when you were eighteen-years-old," he concluded.

Just to put Shearer's twenty-five year career with *The Simpsons* into perspective, from around 1989 up until 1998 he was paid $30,000 per episode, then after the show became a wild success and renegotiating his contract, this jumped to $125,000. His income then jumped again to $250,000 an episode a few years later. In 2008 he was being paid $400,000 per episode, but he and other *Simpsons* staff had to take a pay cut in 2013 in order to lower production costs of the show or else Fox was going to cancel it, so his pay was reduced to $300,000 per episode.[165]

So Shearer himself is just as wealthy as some of the Bohemian Grove members, and being part of Hollywood's elite means he probably has a lot more in common with the men inside the Bohemian Grove than he does with the average American.

---

[165] *The Washington Post* "Harry Shearer, voice of Mr. Burns, to leave 'The Simpsons,' reports say" by Justin Moyer (May 14th 2015)

Lucy, Daughter of the Devil

The Turner Broadcasting Network (TBN) owns the Cartoon Network—which, as its name suggests—consists of cartoons primarily for kids, but after primetime, when most children are supposed to be in bed, the network changes its format to what they call "Adult Swim" and airs raunchy cartoons supposedly aimed at adults. One such show called *Lucy, Daughter of the Devil* was a short ten minute CGI comedy about Satan trying to convince his daughter, Lucy, to fulfill her role as the Antichrist.

In 2007 an episode titled "Human Sacrifice" was about a satanic ritual at the Bohemian Grove which was being performed to honor a senator who had been chosen to be elected as the next president. "Chosen to be elected," meaning the elite members control the elections through fraud and had chosen him to be their next puppet.[166]

A character named DJ Jesús, who is Jesus Christ—and Lucy's boyfriend in the show, was chosen as the person to be sacrificed to celebrate the new president being picked. Jesus was lured to the Bohemian Grove under the pretense that he would be DJing a party that will be like the film *Eyes Wide Shut* and is told that Alan Greenspan

---

[166] See *Hacking Democracy* (2006) produced by HBO

(former chairman of the Federal Reserve Bank) will be there.

The Bohemian Grove, as depicted in the cartoon, is clearly modeled after the actual Grove and includes the giant owl statue with the altar at its feet and men wearing hooded robes holding flaming torches—all identical to the real Bohemian Grove. "Half of Washington" is in attendance in the episode and everyone chants "Hail Satan" as the ritual begins. The Devil even boasts that ten presidents have announced their candidacy in the Bohemian Grove as the ceremony begins.

Before he can be killed, DJ Jesús escapes and the episode ends by zooming out to an aerial view showing the location of the incident being in Northern California, where the actual Grove is located.

Conclusion

After sixty years of mainstream media blackouts regarding the elusive and secretive Bilderberg Group, it became impossible in the age of social media and smartphones to keep them under wraps any longer. The easily swallowed claims of the Bilderberg Group being "just another business conference," are now offered up after the decades of denials about their existence and power, but writing off the Bohemian Grove as "just another party" is not so easy.

Most of the public gullibly buy into the claims now that the Bilderberg Group is just a bunch of men in suits getting together for another boring meeting, but trying to explain the Cremation of Care—not to mention the allegations of Satanism and child abuse that hang over the Bohemian Grove—is quite a bit more difficult. The video footage and photos of the annual "human sacrifice" ceremony would be disturbing to most people once they saw it, and no amount of whitewash or spin would remove the suspicions that many have about the Bohemian Grove.

A bunch of guys meeting for a three-day conference in the case of the Bilderberg Group is pretty easy to brush off as something rather normal—a bunch of men gathering in the middle of a secluded forest, dressing up in hooded robes, and engaging in a "human sacrifice" ritual—not so much.

Even setting this aside, it's clear that the Bohemian Grove serves as an elite consensus-building party, held about a month after the more formal Bilderberg conference which occurs in the late spring each year. If one wants to gain a comprehensive view of the world and the mechanisms of power that work to guide it, then learning about the Bohemian Grove is a critical piece of the puzzle.

As Mary Moore of the Bohemian Grove Action Network once said, "Kiwanis and Rotary clubs in every small town has that same sort of 'good-old-boy network' of prominent men in the community getting to know each other through a social club. But when you get to the level of the Bohemian Grove, it's a very global network, and much more powerful."[167]

When the wealthiest and most powerful men in the world, from heads of industry to high ranking government officials and those who work in the intelligence agencies, all meet together to hang out and listen to off the record lectures given by a variety of experts and insiders, it is

---

[167] *SonomaCountyFreePress.org* (website now defunct)

undeniable that this has a tremendous impact on society as a whole.

At the time I'm finishing writing this in June of 2015, very few books exist on the Bohemian Grove, and most Americans have still never heard of it. The stories are so strange that even when they do, many dismiss them as an Internet urban legend or a conspiracy theory, but you now hold the evidence in your hands.

I hope this book has helped shed some light on this dark subject, and put some of the wild allegations into their proper context so you can understand where they came from and why they spread. If you would like to continue your education on related subjects, I encourage you to checkout some of my previous books, and if it's not too much to ask, please write a brief (or lengthy) review for this one and rate it on Amazon.com or whatever e-bookstore you downloaded it from to let other potential readers know what you think.

Please pass this book on to someone else now that you have finished it to share the information with them, and thanks again for investing your time and energy into my ten-year-long investigation of *The Bohemian Grove: Facts & Fiction*.

Further Reading

The Illuminati: Facts & Fiction

Secret societies have both fascinated and frightened people for hundreds of years. Often the infamous Illuminati is mentioned as the core of conspiracies which span the globe. The Illuminati is actually a historical secret society which had goals of revolutions and world domination dating back to the 1770s.

Since then, rumors and conspiracy theories involving the Illuminati continue to spread, sometimes finding their way into popular novels like Dan Brown's *Angels & Demons* and Hollywood movies like *Lara Croft: Tomb Raider*. Some men have even come forward claiming to be former members, offering details of what they allege are the inner workings of the organization. When you sift through all of the information available on the subject, you may be surprised that the truth is stranger than fiction.

In *The Illuminati: Facts & Fiction*, conspiracy and occult expert Mark Dice separates history from Hollywood and shows why tales of the secret society won't die.

The New World Order: Facts & Fiction

What is the New World Order? Proponents say that it's an anticipated new era of global cooperation between diverse nations and cultures aimed at ushering in a utopia providing all the earth's citizens with everything they need.

Detractors claim it's the systematic take-over by secret societies, quasi-government entities and corporations who are covertly organizing a global socialist all-powerful government which aims to regulate every aspect of citizens' lives, rendering them a perpetual working-class while the elite leadership lives in luxury.

Conspiracy theory expert Mark Dice looks at the evidence, claims, and conspiracy theories as he takes you down the rabbit hole to *The New World Order*.

- *Calls for a New World Order*
- *World Governed Through Secret Societies*
- *Mainstream Media Controlled by the Elite*
- *Banking, Money, and Taxes*
- *One World Currency*
- *Population Reduction*
- *One World Religion*
- *A Coming Global Dictator Who Will Claim to be God*

Illuminati in the Music Industry

Famous pop stars and rappers from Jay-Z and Rick Ross to Rihanna and Christina Aguilera are believed by many to be a part of the infamous Illuminati secret society. These stars allegedly use Illuminati and satanic symbolism in their music videos and on their clothes that goes unnoticed by those not "in the know."

Since these stars appear in our livings rooms on family friendly mainstream shows like Good Morning America, Ellen, and dozens of others—and are loved by virtually all the kids—they couldn't possibly have anything to do with the infamous Illuminati or anything "satanic," could they? Some famous musicians have even publicly denounced the Illuminati in interviews or songs.

Illuminati in the Music Industry takes a close look at some of today's hottest stars and decodes the secret symbols, song lyrics, and separates the facts from the fiction in this fascinating topic. You may never see your favorite musicians the same way ever again.

Big Brother: The Orwellian Nightmare Come True

In *Big Brother*, Mark Dice details actual high-tech spy gadgets, mind-reading machines, government projects, and emerging artificial intelligence systems that seem as if they came right out of George Orwell's novel *Nineteen Eighty-Four*.

Orwell's famous book was first published in 1949, and tells the story of a nightmarish future where citizens have lost all privacy and are continuously monitored by the omniscient Big Brother surveillance system which keeps them obedient to a totalitarian government.

The novel is eerily prophetic as many of the fictional systems of surveillance described have now become a reality. Mark Dice shows you the scary documentation that Big Brother is watching you, and is more powerful than you could imagine.

- *Orwellian Government Programs*
- *Facial Recognition Scanners*
- *Mind Reading Machines*
- *Neural Interfaces*
- *Psychotronic Weapons*
- *The Nanny State*
- *Artificial Intelligence*
- *Cybernetic Organisms*

The Resistance Manifesto

The Resistance Manifesto by Mark Dice contains 450 pages of extensively researched and documented information drawing from declassified documents, mainstream news articles, religious texts, and personal interviews. A dark web of evil is exposed like never before, making Bible Prophecy and the New World Order crystal clear.

Learn the most powerful information about the Illuminati, plans for the rise of the Antichrist, the institutions, people, and powers involved, and how you can fight them.

"Powerful and compelling. A must read."
- Alex Jones from Infowars.com

"Mark takes you beyond 9/11 into a world of secret societies, mystics, and madmen."
- Jason Bermas, Producer of *Loose Change*

"Mark Dice is not a conspiracy theorist, he is a conspiracy realist. This book tells it like it is. I urge every American to read it and pass it on to your friends and relatives. Wake up America!"
- Ted Gunderson, Senior Special Agent in Charge (retired) FBI Los Angeles

Inside the Illuminati

When looking into the existence and alleged activities of the infamous Illuminati secret society, one finds an overwhelming amount of conspiracy theories, hidden history, half-truths and hoaxes.

But how much truth is there to some of these claims? What is the real history of the mysterious group? Do they continue to exist today? What is the evidence? And what are they doing?

After a decade of research sifting through the facts and the fiction, secret society expert Mark Dice will help you navigate through the complex maze from the original documents to rare revelations from elite politicians, bankers and businessmen, as he takes you *Inside the Illuminati.*

- *Insider Revelations*
- *Original Writings*
- *Spiritual Beliefs*
- *Occult Symbolism*
- *Early Evidence*
- *Zodiac Club*
- *"Ex Members"*
- *Communism*
- *Seraphic Society*
- *The Jesuits*
- *The Jasons*
- *And more!*

The Bilderberg Group: Facts & Fiction

Every spring since 1954, a group of approximately one hundred of the world's most powerful businessmen, politicians, media moguls, and international royalty meet in secret for several days to discuss the course of the world. Called the Bilderberg Group after the Bilderberg Hotel in Oosterbeck, Holland where their first meeting was held, this off the record annual gathering is said to be where the globalist puppet masters plot and scheme.

Does this group of power elite develop new political, economic, and cultural policies that are then covertly implemented by their underlings? Do they choose who our world leaders will be, including the next president of the United States? Is the Bilderberg Group a shadow government? Are they the Illuminati? Why has the mainstream media had a complete blackout regarding their meetings for decades? Who attends? And who pays for it?

Is this "just another conference?" Or, are the "conspiracy theorists" right? What is the evidence? How were they first discovered? What are they doing? And should the public be concerned? Secret society expert Mark Dice will show you the hidden history, financial records, and some of the insider leaks showing how this small group's consensus has staggering effects on the political landscape of the world, global economies, wars, and more, as he uncovers *The Bilderberg Group: Facts & Fiction.*

- *Their History*
- *Bilderberg's Goals*
- *Their Discovery*
- *Recent Meetings*
- *Members and Guests*
- *Actions and Effects*
- *Financial Records*
- *The Oath of Silence*
- *Media Blackouts*
- *Exclusive Photos*
- *And More!*

About the Author

Mark Dice is a media analyst, author, and political activist who, in an entertaining and educational way, gets people to question our celebrity obsessed culture and the role the mainstream media and elite secret societies play in shaping our lives.

Mark's YouTube channel has received over 100 million views and his viral videos have been mentioned on ABC's *The View*, the Fox News Channel, CNN, the *Drudge Report*, *TMZ*, the *New York Daily News*, the *Washington Post,* and other media outlets around the world.

He has been featured on various television shows including the History Channel's *Decoded, Ancient Aliens,* and *America's Book of Secrets; Conspiracy Theory with Jesse Ventura, Secret Societies of Hollywood* on E! Channel, *America Declassified* on the Travel Channel, and is a frequent guest on *Coast to Coast AM*, *The Alex Jones Show*, and more.

Mark Dice is the author of several popular books on secret societies and conspiracies, including *The Illuminati: Facts & Fiction, Big Brother: The Orwellian Nightmare Come True, The New World Order: Facts & Fiction, The Bilderberg Group: Facts & Fiction, The*

Resistance Manifesto, Illuminati in the Music Industry, and *Inside the Illuminati*, which are all available in paperback on Amazon.com or e-book on Kindle, iBooks, Nook or Google Play.

While much of Mark's work confirms the existence and continued operation of the Illuminati today, he is also dedicated to debunking conspiracy theories and hoaxes and separating the facts from the fiction; hence the "Facts & Fiction" subtitle for several of his books.

While having respect for all authentic religions and belief systems, Mark Dice is a Christian and holds a bachelor's degree in communication from California State University. He lives in San Diego, California.

He enjoys causing trouble for the New World Order, exposing corrupt scumbag politicians, and pointing out Big Brother's prying eyes. The term "fighting the New World Order" is used by Mark to describe some of his activities, and refers to his and others' resistance and opposition (*The Resistance*) to the overall system of political corruption, illegal wars, elite secret societies, mainstream media, Big Brother and privacy issues; as well as various economic and social issues. This Resistance involves self-improvement, self-sufficiency, personal responsibility and spiritual growth.

Made in United States
Troutdale, OR
07/13/2023

11189850R00102